W9-CBC-768

The
Human Side of
Management

———

The
Human Side of
Management

*Management by Integration
and Self-Control*

George S. Odiorne

Lexington Books
D.C. Heath and Company/Lexington, Massachusetts/Toronto

in association with

University Associates, Inc.
San Diego, California

93440

Library of Congress Cataloging-in-Publication Data

Odiorne, George S.
The human side of management.

Bibliography: p.
Includes index.
1. Management by objectives.   2. Personnel
management.   3. Employees, Training of.   4. Job
enrichment.   I. Title.
HD30.65.035   1987   658.3   86-46314
ISBN 0-669-15350-8 (alk. paper)

Published simultaneously in Canada
Printed in the United States of America
Casebound International Standard Book Number: 0-669-15350-8
Library of Congress Catalog Card Number: 86-46314

The paper used in this publication meets the minimum requirements of
American National Standard for Information Sciences—Permanance
of Paper for Printed Library Materials, ANSI Z39.48-1984.

87 88 89 90 8 7 6 5 4 3 2 1

Contents

viii   *The Human Side of Management*

Preface

The title of this book, as many will recognize, is a variation on the title of Douglas McGregor's classic book, *The Human Side of Enterprise,* written in the 1950s and published in 1960. This book's subtitle, *Management by Integration and Self-Control,* was the title of one of the chapters in McGregor's book.

About thirty years ago, the Alfred P. Sloan Foundation funded a study by professors Alex Bavelas and Douglas McGregor of the School of Industrial Management at the Massachusetts Institute of Technology. The basic issue: Is a successful manager born or made? The question, originally posed by Mr. Sloan, was pursued along different routes by the two professors. Bavelas, who was a sociologist and an experimentalist, explored the subject through laboratory experiments. Douglas McGregor, who was decidedly not an experimentalist, focused his attention upon how management development programs work and whether they actually produce good managers. His conclusions? That such programs really don't achieve all they hope, or even very much at all. A more general conclusion by McGregor, however, as a by-product, became his book, *The Human Side of Enterprise.* The main thesis of that work was a division of managerial assumptions about human behavior into two major classifications, Theory X and Theory Y. Theory X, McGregor said, assumes that "the average human being has an inherent dislike of work and will avoid it if he can," and thus must be controlled, intimidated, or coerced to get him to produce. Theory Y makes an opposite assumption about the nature of people. The average person, goes Theory Y, finds work "as natural as play or rest." Thus he can be relied upon for self-control, given a commitment to suitable goals and related rewards for achievement.

In line with that assumption, McGregor proposed that manager performance appraisals and decisions about pay and promotion centering on performance should be based on "management by integration and self-control." In a subsequent article in *Harvard Business Review,* McGregor said that the system then being used for manager appraisal at General Mills, known as "management by objectives," was a practical application of this ideal. Since I was at that time the personnel manager at General Mills, responsible for the operation of this system, I was thoroughly in agreement with McGregor.

Peter Drucker, in his best-selling book, *The Practice of Management* (1954), had proposed a system he called "management by objectives and self-control." As a graduate student under Drucker at the New York University Graduate School of Business, I had heard him expound upon this approach, which he declared was the basis for much of the managerial success of General Motors, where Drucker had been a consultant to Sloan. It stimulated me to study and refine the system further, and to publish in 1965 my first book, with the title *Management by Objectives: A System of Managerial Leadership.* Much of my subsequent research, writing, and teaching has been the development of management by objectives (MBO).

Since its beginning, MBO has become pervasive, albeit controversial, in large organizations. For some critics, writers, and managers, Theory Y became a general rubric for every kind of soft or sentimental employee-contentment plan ever created. In McGregor's original definition it means management by integration and self-control.

Edward Locke of the University of Maryland must be credited with the first and most important body of rigorous empirical research into the effectiveness of MBO. Many others studied the conditions under which it worked—or failed. Today a majority of the largest corporations, banks, hospitals, and government agencies use some form of MBO as their management system. Whether or not they do it well—its scope and completeness of use varies widely—there is no doubt that MBO has become orthodox management theory. No strategic plan could stand without first defining overall organization objectives for a multiyear span of time. The idea that bosses will talk to subordinates about the subordinates' objectives, rather than simply dictating them, is even more widely supported.

At the same time it must be admitted that not everyone who has embraced MBO has been as ardent in adopting the integration and self-control aspect. Many organizations with hard-nosed management use only management by objectives, with the goals being defined at the top and passed down. In such firms, the philosophy and system of integration and self-control are still to be tried.

Since the early 1970s I have written and published a newsletter dealing with the executive skills required to operate a goals-driven organization. Thousands of American and foreign managers read the *Odiorne Newsletter* and have communicated with me about their practices and findings. The idea for a book using mainly materials incorporated originally in the newsletter was proposed by William Pfeiffer, the forward-thinking president of University Associates. Thomas Kleber, editor and publisher of the *Odiorne Newsletter,* deserves great credit for making those newsletters coherent. Richard Roe of University Associates has been a constant source of encouragement and support. His staff, including Bob Nelson and the marketing staff, with their encouragement to "write something which will be close to the readers," exemplify the best kind of support an author could hope for.

The results contained in this book must, however, be considered wholly my responsibility, including lapses, oversights, shortcomings, and omissions.

Douglas McGregor has passed away, but his admirers and disciples are legion. He was thoroughly convinced of the merits of integration and self-control and never hesitated to admonish me against overselling the concept of goals without the participation of subordinates, a warning many practitioners often forget. While MBO as a program or package plan for managing and appraising managers has occasionally been turned into a bureaucratic procedure bordering upon a cookbook recipe, the basic idea of integration and self-control is stronger now than ever. This is in part because the world, and especially the work force, of the eighties is radically changed. There are more professionals, more college graduates, more women, more minorities, and more middle-class people in the work force now. White-collar jobs clearly outnumber blue-collar jobs. The U.S. economy has become more service-based, and today's jobs are more likely to be information-producing than industrial-goods-producing. While McGregor was properly concerned in the late fifties with the problems of the factory work force and the motivation of laborers, the major concern today is upon managing the "knowledge worker"—the well-educated and highly talented white-collar worker. Yet it is exactly this emergence of an information-producing society staffed by knowledge workers that has made McGregor's approach even more relevant than it was in his own day.

This book is divided into four parts. Basic principles of management and of setting goals to achieve integration and self-control are spelled out in Parts I and II. Part III delves into productivity, training, and management development. Part IV highlights mentoring and commitment. Though, like McGregor and Drucker, I am not an experimentalist, I have attempted to incorporate the best work of experimentalists and researchers, and references are cited for each chapter. The style is narrative and anecdotal rather than explanatory and scientific, and the practitioner and scholar may find that it is more prescriptive than would suit the taste of the research-centered behavioral scientist. It is the trainer, the management development specialist, and the operating manager for whom this book is written.

Special appreciation goes to Rose Marie Karkheck of Eckerd College for the final typing, revising, and make-up of the finished manuscript.

The
Human Side of
Management

———

Part I
Managing Managers as a Resource

A tourist driving along a country road in Vermont ran over a farmer's cat. Appalled, he sought out the farmer and confessed that he had killed the unfortunate animal. "Is there anything I can do?" he asked. The farmer paused for a moment, then replied, "How are you at catching mice?"

The moral: *Good results come ahead of good intentions.*

1
Managers as a Source—and Resource

How well managers manage and are managed determines whether business goals will be reached.

—Peter Drucker

A couple of years ago I read that the average length of life of a business in this country is seven years. The reason? According to this source, bad management accounts for 92.5 percent of these lamentable failures.

This high rate of business failures is familiar to every banker who has been stuck with a bad business loan. Even the casual visitor to any modern shopping center can verify the rapid rate of turnover. The boutique, restaurant, food store, or small high-fashion shop that started off with fanfares and high hopes often won't be there when you visit the same center next year. Along the highways around Boston, central North Carolina, Palo Alto, and other high-tech centers, the casualty rate is equally high. The brilliant scientist with a clever idea for a new product flourishes until his start-up capital is gone, and then he folds his tent and steals away. Even the largest firms aren't immune from this apparently inexorable failure rate. An impressive list of firms whose names were household words ten years ago no longer exist today. Some, like W.T. Grant, have gone into Chapter 11—bankruptcy. Others are bought at bargain prices by companies that take over the people, products, and markets of the businesses. In other cases—probably a majority—the saddened entrepreneurs simply walk away from the whole thing, without even enough cash left in their checking accounts to file for bankruptcy. The creditors shrug and write off their losses. This high business failure rate isn't due to acts of God, but of managers.

But managers are also the people who build great empires, create new dynasties, and engineer giant, multibillion-dollar mergers. R.J. Reynolds, once a cigarette company, has grown into a multibillion-dollar multibusiness giant through acquiring other giant corporations such as Standard Brands, Heublein, and the like. Wells Fargo Bank moved into the upper echelons of the banking industry by acquiring Crocker Bank. Philip Morris now owns General Foods; Marriott owns Howard Johnson; and on and on. It is managers at the top of the organization who design and orchestrate these giant mergers.

In still other cases, companies, plants, and nonprofit organizations that were once failing turn around and become flourishing and successful again. The story of the turnaround at Chrysler Corporation under the management of Lee Iacocca is a modern business legend.

What are the qualities of managers who can make such dramatic alterations in the way organizations function? The number of questions and the amount of speculation about the difference between successful and unsuccessful managers is endless. As Albert Camus stated about knowledge in general: "That which is important we can never know for sure, and that which we know for sure isn't really important." What we really know for sure is that the successful manager is a manager who is successful, and the unsuccessful manager is a manager who is unsuccessful. Furthermore, the unsuccessful manager of yesterday or yesteryear may be the managerial superstar of today, and today's hero in management may be tomorrow's goat.

The search for answers to the unresolved problems in managing managers goes on. What kinds of people should we choose? Who shall rise in the organization? How should rewards be dispensed? Similar practical questions are both necessary and recurring. They require that decisions be made whether we know the answers or we don't. All of these decisions require that we rely upon some theory of management and some criteria which delineate good from bad performance. It is precisely in the question of management theory that we discover the greatest disagreement among qualified experts about managerial abilities, qualities, behavior, actions, and systems.

A Jungle of Theories

The business world has not been lacking in theories to explain the complex job of the executive. Often these explanations have been mutually exclusive, and often they've been rooted in the biases and expertise of the explainer rather than in hard evidence of what top executives really do. The late Harold Koontz of UCLA referred to the "theory jungle," which may be helpful as an overall description but does little to clarify the nature of the executive territory for the person who enters it. *P239*

Some of the prevailing kinds of theories include the following:

The Classic Functions of Management

Henri Fayol, a French industrialist, looking back in 1930 upon his own varied and successful career, declared that in any business there is a body of knowledge called management that is separate and distinct from the activity being managed. He then went on to identify several management functions such as organizing, planning, coordinating, and controlling.

Between 1930 and 1950 a school of management functions theorists emerged, viewing the corporation as some sort of ponderous machine with fixed rules and principles which must be applied for efficiency. This comprised the basis of management as a separate topic which ultimately flowered into an academic department in business schools.

Ralph C. Davis summed up these theories in 1951 into an integrated whole, settling for organizing, planning, and controlling as the three most vital functions which were to be melded into a leadership pattern through such concepts as authority, responsibility, and accountability.

Behavioral Theories

The initial intrusion of the social and behavioral sciences into management theory was brought about largely through some experiments conducted in the Hawthorne plant of Western Electric in

1927. Social scientists from Harvard were invited in to conduct experiments to explain the causes of high and low productivity of workers. Their conclusion, that social and psychological factors in the workplace itself were of utmost importance, constituted a denial of certain long-held assumptions about what motivates the workers, or what causes high productivity. In the past it had been presumed that this was based solely upon a single-minded search for financial rewards.

The Hawthorne studies in turn led to numerous other behavioral studies, not only of the motivation of workers but also of the nature of organizational behavior and the functioning of groups. This research as it emerged focused upon three aspects of behavior: that of individuals, that of groups, and that of complex organizations.

For the behavioral sciences, this new field of research—studying the last undiscovered native tribe—was a bonanza. Tiring of experiments with rabbits, rats, pigeons, and primates, the behavioral scientists now turned their attention to executives with a zeal nearly matched by the enthusiasm of the executives themselves for being studied.

The job of administration is seen by the behavioral school as one of choosing arrangements which will evoke a system of cooperative relationships between the people who are to accomplish the goals of the organization. To put this approach to work, managers must become talented amateurs in applied psychology, sociology, and even anthropology.

Management Science

During World War II researchers from the physical and mathematical sciences developed approaches to the management job which proposed that mathematical analysis, model building, and sophisticated operations research were the keys to effective management. Based upon a systematic study of decision making, the management science movement requires that managers use the systems approach to manage the organization.

The mathematical model which is at the heart of this approach has been assisted materially by the rapidly growing use of computers to simulate decisions in advance to improve their quality and avoid the effects of failure. Several societies and journals for professionals in management science, operations research, and systems approaches have emerged since 1950.

Scientific Management

Even earlier, some U.S. engineers had turned their attention to the tasks of management and produced a body of knowledge known as scientific management. Widely popular during the early part of the century, scientific management was centered around the work of Frederick Taylor, an engineer, and consists of four key elements: (1) developing the best way of doing each job; (2) selecting and developing workers; (3) matching workers with jobs; and (4) obtaining close cooperation between managers and workers.

It was this approach which ultimately led to a more scientific and rigorous analysis of the tasks of workers, and also led in part to the creation of industrial engineering as a profession. Scientific management is still widely used in mass-production industries today, although it has been modified by some of the more modern approaches.

Situational Management

If the result of all these conflicting theories is confusion on the part of the emergent manager as to what is actually done by successful executives, this should come as no surprise. In effect the theory jungle suggests that the executive must be a combination scientist, systems expert, industrial engineer, psychologist, sociologist, and administrator.

But even if the chief executive were to be a complete master of all these competing theories and were to know when to apply which one, this would result only in his or her being qualified to teach management courses in a college, not necessarily to run a large organization. Few managers at the top are guided consciously by any theory. They are guided by practicality.

Descriptions of executive skills, often grimly sober, proliferate steadily. There are even some writers who suggest that most of these theories are irrelevant. Henry Mintzberg of McGill University, for example, has expressed serious doubt that managers actually engage in the kinds of behavior attributed to them in theory. Likewise, Edward Wrapp asserts that managers are more likely to "wheel and deal" than to follow any systematic pattern of learned behavior.

Situational management may be the prevailing theory of management in practice today. This is an attempt to reconcile the conflicting theories and descriptions by identifying managerial behavior as being solidly rooted in the precept "It all depends." Upon what does it depend? The company, its people, the environment, the rate of growth or decline, the age and stability of the industry, the amount of government regulation which is confronted, the amount and quality of competition, and a thousand other possible variables.

This leaves only a few constants for the manager to watch and adhere to: Define the goals clearly, and be adaptive in reacting to whatever comes. The style and behavior of situational leaders are discussed in chapter 3. In effect, situational management means setting goals and then working hard to accomplish them.

The Manager as Trustee

A rash of governmental regulations and a rising environmental movement during the sixties and seventies made executives aware that they needed to cater to a lot more than the interests of stockholders or unions. In fact, the new theory went, the manager is simply a trustee for a number of different groups, many of which are competing for management's favor.

In this theory, a major element of the senior executive's job is the corporation's responsibility to its various constituencies—stockholders, employees and their unions, customers, and the general public. Although there are certainly more than four groups, these are commonly accepted as the major ones:

1. *Stockholders* today are most likely to be pension fund trustees, bank trust officers, mutual fund managers, insurance company investment officers, or similar large-portfolio managers. Such people are sophisticated investors, keenly interested in the details of the business in which they hold stocks. Portfolio managers are espe-

cially aware of any influences inside the firm, the industry, or the economy that could adversely affect the value of their investment. They are also quick to dispose of a company's stock if its earnings have fallen or if there is a threat that they might fall. As trustees of the assets of their clients, they have a legal obligation as well as professional pride in holding only those assets which promise to grow and which produce earnings. This simple fact of life dominates the world of senior executives. No single crisis or problem can outweigh the endless need for results which affect the wealth of stockholders.

The stewardship role of the executive is blurred when the pension funds of a company's employees actually own significant amounts of the company's stock. They become even more blurred when the employees buy out the company, as has happened in a number of industries in recent years.

No amount of financial public relations can relieve the top executives of the pressing concern of stockholders, but this is not the end of a senior executive's concerns.

2. *Employees and their unions* have certain rights and interests which must be protected. The right to organize for purposes of collective bargaining over wages, hours, and working conditions is protected by law. The employer is required to bargain in good faith with duly chosen agents of the workers, to reduce agreements to written contract form, and to abide by the terms of these contracts. Numerous other laws govern the labor/management relationship: Union-busting activities are illegal. Minimum wages must be paid. Safe working conditions are mandatory. Unemployment insurance must be provided in the event of necessary discharge of workers. In addition, the firm cannot discriminate against women and minorities in hiring, pay, promotions, and supervision.

3. *Customers* are protected against defective or ineffective products and have a right to believe that the claims of the company for its products are reliable and believable. Products in certain crucial categories, such as drugs, must pass the registration and approval procedures of government regulatory agencies, and if found defective may be recalled at the expense of the manufacturing corporation.

4. *The public* is likewise protected from wrongful and harmful

behavior on the part of the corporation. Under environmental protection laws, a firm may not create a cesspool of polluted air and water as an ordinary way of making its products, and if it does it must remedy those evils. The protection of the public extends to acts by corporations which are careless, inept, and stupid as well as those which are merely venal and greedy. In addition it is expected that the corporation will obey all of the criminal laws; if it doesn't, it can be indicted and punished like any individual. Corporations often cannot engage in "diverse treatment," favoring one group over another in its works, and often must divulge their business records to government agencies seeking to uncover peccadilloes and sins of omission as well as sins of commission.

As the ladder-climbing manager undergoes early training, the pressures of job objectives and demands for specific performance may often make these trustee relationships seem academic and remote. The manager of a copper refinery or a coal mine finds that the pressure for tonnage is often in conflict with environmental laws, and under such pressure learns to treat the trustee function as an inconvenience, if not a downright nuisance. Once at the top, however, the need to achieve both goals becomes part of the job. Early experience is often poor preparation for this trustee responsibility; it is not surprising that many managers attempt to ignore or circumvent this role.

Since life in the pressure-cooker heat of immediate goals at lower ranks doesn't prepare one very well for a world in which long-range, externally originated matters are of great concern, rising managerial stars often find the climate at the top to be quite different from what they had expected.

Where does this leave the modern manager? Harlan Cleveland, in his book *The Knowledge Executive*, writes that "the executive weaves and dodges among his or her constituencies persuading, cajoling, lobbying, budgeting, arbitrating, bargaining, fund raising, trying to keep cool in the management of contradiction." Although this description is probably truer in university settings where Cleveland spent much of his time, it has many elements of truth for the corporate executive in a world of environmentalists, legislators, directors, trustees, and public gadflies. While the subject of top executives, their lives, their habits, and their idiosyncrasies is certainly the object of more attention than that of the project manager, the foreman, or the field sales supervisor, an executive's major forte must be the management of people. Furthermore, as McGregor asserted and the theme of this book expands, the trend of the eighties and nineties will be specifically toward integrating people and managing them through self-control.

The greatest number of managers work in the lower levels of management. Supervision of most workers falls upon the three million or more people who are identified as first-line management. In the eyes of the law, they are the first level with the power "to hire, fire, suspend, promote, demote, or effectively recommend." They are exempt from the Fair Labor Standards Act by virtue of their managerial roles. It is this group—the core resource—that upper management must learn to manage.

2
Supervision: The Key to Integration

Officials and other administrative employees do not own the resources
necessary for the performance of their assigned functions but they are
accountable for their use of these resources.

—Max Weber

O ne of the more popular definitions of management is that it
consists of getting results through other people. The supervisor in an administrative position must direct people toward organization goals, using technology and resources which are under his
or her control. The world of administration and management can
thus be divided into the order-givers and the order-takers. Traditionally, the orders flow down and then the reports flow upward.
Yet, in this time of better educated workers, often it is the workers
who have the greater knowledge and experience about the jobs they
do. Orders made from ignorance to workers having the bulk of the
knowledge are ill advised if not counterproductive.

Just as with management theories in general, the character and
role of the leader in supervisory management has several alternative
explanations. Some say personal traits, identifiable characteristics,
or psychological properties are what makes a person a leader. Others deny this approach in favor of a supportive leadership theory in
which the supervisor is characterized by supportive, democratic,
employee-centered leadership. Such a leadership style is more con-
siderate of followers. Still others see the supervisor as an instrument
of the bureaucracy who executes such standardized functions as organizing, planning, and controlling the work of subordinates and
order-takers. Max Weber proposed that some leaders possess cha-
risma, a magical kind of leadership quality.

The most widely accepted leadership theory today is that of the
situational leader. This is the leader whose behavior is multidimen-

sional and whose style varies according to the situation. These dimensions include the personality of the leader, the technical requirements of tasks to be performed by the leader and the followers, and the social, cultural, and physical environment in which the leader and the followers operate.

Fred Fiedler is generally credited as the father of the situational leadership theory, which he based upon twelve years' research with more than twenty-five major studies. Three situational components were considered to be basic:

1. Clearly structured and defined tasks which can be delegated and controlled by members of the organization.

2. Some legal authority to enforce the will of the leader upon the organization's members.

3. A personal relationship between the leader and members of his or her group that produces support from the group.

A World of Difference

Supervision is the direction and leadership of a group of immediate followers. The president of the firm supervises a small handful of vice presidents. Clearly the vice presidents have power and authority in their own right, but their immediate boss is the president, and for them he is the supervisor. At the other end of the organization a leader may supervise a roomful of assemblers, for whom that person is supervisor. Supervision is distinguished from the nature of overall organizational leadership by the immediacy of the contact and reporting relationship.

Studies by the National Opinion Research Corporation (NORC) of people's attitudes toward their company and, even more important, general attitudes toward the whole system of free enterprise, found that the level of satisfaction within the world of business is often related to the level of satisfaction a person has with his or her immediate supervision and job. In other words, if you have a good boss, you are more likely to think that the system is okay. If you have a bad boss or are otherwise dissatisfied with your immediate job, you will tend to extend that discontent to larger spheres.

A study using this NORC data was conducted by Professor Arie Reichel. He divided the sample population into two groups—people who have high trust in big business and the people who run it, and people who have low trust in the same groups. The high-trust group felt that what they say counts, that they have prestigious occupations, and that the people in charge of the country care about them. (They also report watching very little television.)

On the other hand, people with low trust in big business and the people who run it are characterized by a feeling of powerlessness. They regard their occupations as low in prestige, feel alienated politically from the national scene, believe they are underpaid, and are dissatisfied with their work. (They, incidentally, watch more television than members of the satisfied group.)

The implications of this study for social stability and for further governmental control of large organizations are considerable. An angry, apathetic, and alienated work force means that productivity—in goods or services—is certain to suffer. The quality of work goes down.

The behavior of the supervisor under whom people work can make a world of difference in the quality of their jobs. People who have an opportunity to discuss job objectives and job plans with their supervisors, people whose supervisors use systems and exhibit behavior which is in tune with the employees' needs and values, people whose supervisors integrate the employees into the organization will have higher levels of job satisfaction than those employees denied such things.

For the employer responsible for designing supervisory jobs, such information is crucial. Because first-line supervisors constitute the largest management group, it is upon them that the onus of proper supervision falls first.

It is exactly in this design of the supervisory system that the "situation" within which the supervisor operates is created. Company policy, disciplinary practices, methods of setting goals and reviewing results, how employees are paid—all are an integral part of this system. It may be possible that a good supervisor could overcome the effects of a bad system. Geary Rummler, however, suggests that if you "pit a good person against a bad system, the system will win"—if not every time, at least most of the time.

Traditional practices of supervision under Theory X assumptions have assumed that pay was the most significant, if not the only source of alienation. It's true that data shows that lower-paid people are the most alienated, and that the highest paid are often less alienated. This doesn't automatically mean that pay is the only factor, but that it may be an incidental or concurrent condition of dissatisfaction. There are more than enough examples of people whose pay is not very high but who are extremely satisfied with their role, their work, and the system overall. Teachers, welfare workers, priests and ministers, and other caring professionals often work at well below the level of pay of other professionals. Schoolteachers, for example, receive about half the pay of a truck driver, plumber, carpenter, or machinist, but studies show a high level of accomplishment and satisfaction—despite systematic aggravations from above. Their vision of the future, expressed through teaching future generations, seems to be impervious to the strongest efforts of administrators and school boards to subvert such sentiments.

The Supervisor as Integrator

For the organization which hopes to achieve management by integration and self-control, supervisory practices would thus appear to be an excellent place to start. Even though the behavior and attitude of the workers in an organization flow from the system and its information, and from the training they have received in preparation for their job, the supervisor orchestrates the way in which the system affects the worker. Supervisors can be integrators or alienators.

During the late seventies a rash of books and articles about the purported superiority of Japanese management and supervisory systems appeared in the United States. From such supervisory systems, it was declared, has come a work force so superior in quality and productivity that it is able to outproduce the world. Unfortunately, events during the eighties have taken much of the luster off the Japanese model. Japan's steel industry is now languishing. Its textile industry moved to Southeast Asia. Other indicators—including declining productivity—have emerged to erase some of the halo effect which previously characterized Japan as an ideal.

Nonetheless, the leading Japanese industrial firms do have some noteworthy supervision practices. When these practices were transplanted to the United States (in U.S. factories with U.S. workers making Japanese products), they proved to enhance the integration of workers. The Honda motorcar plant in Marysville, Ohio, has proven that integrative supervisor practices can produce high quality and high productivity if applied with a strong desire to provide for workers' needs in their jobs.

The major gain to be applauded from the recent interest in Japanese management is the new focus which it has brought to the first-line supervisory job. The most lasting impact will probably be the quality circle, a group of people whose work is related and who meet to discuss problems and ideas. Once formed and implemented by some staff department, the quality circle is generally left in the hands of first-line supervisors. The big gain to be realized from this may not be the quality circle itself but the fact that management has once more fastened its eye on a long-neglected problem: building and maintaining a strong corps of first-line managers.

Experienced observers of the manufacturing scene now agree that the role, status, and function of the first-line supervisor is one of the top agenda items affecting the future success of an organization.

While the problems of factory foremanship have been discussed endlessly, some major changes in first-line supervision have occurred, involving nature of the job and the kinds of people who hold that post in most organizations today. Here are some of the ways in which first-line management has changed in the past few decades:

1. The number of workers engaged in manufacturing has declined steadily, to the point where white-collar occupations are now far more prevalent than blue-collar occupations.

2. White-collar workers bring different expectations to the job in terms of supervisory practices than do blue-collar workers.

3. With 80 million of the 100 million workers employed in the United States working in service occupations where work is

less likely to be machine-paced, the use of industrial engineering methods for generating standards of performance is limping along behind.

4. Since much of the control of work and output levels in service occupations is determined by the worker, getting people to want to produce is an increasingly important element in supervision.

5. Different skills and new training are required to produce supervisors who can manage engineers, librarians, staff office professionals, truckers, retail clerks, and the like than are required to produce supervisors who manage assembly-line workers.

6. With many more women and minority people in the work force today, there are new values to be reckoned with in training, motivating, and managing supervisors.

7. A lot of new laws place added constraints on supervisors today. In addition to labor laws affecting bargaining, there are now a host of protected workers, including minorities, women, and the handicapped.

Rethinking the Role of the Supervisor

Present practice in the majority of office and service occupations is simple. You select the best technically competent person, or perhaps the one with the greatest seniority, and make him or her a supervisor when a position opens up. Few supervisors are selected by competitive choice—setting criteria, arraying a host of candidates, and then choosing the best person from among the applicants or nominees.

Selection solely on the basis of technical competence and seniority puts a lot of pressure on new supervisors (and on old ones as well) since they lack supervisory training and, in many cases, aptitude.

Fritz Roethlisberger of Harvard University wrote a classic article many years ago in which he called the foreman a "master and victim of double-talk." The double-talk comes from (1) demands from workers for participation in the decisions affecting them, and (2) pressure from management for increased productivity, higher quality, and lower costs.

Today's supervisor is probably better educated—in the sense of formal schooling—than his or her predecessor was, but that education doesn't prepare most people for the actual work of supervision except in remote ways. Where training is provided, in most cases it has been designed and planned by behavioral scientists who have a model in mind which may or may not be relevant to the kind of climate in which the supervisor actually works.

My own studies of some leading firms that have paid serious attention to the status, function, and role of the supervisor show that there are three major categories of responsibilities which comprise the key building blocks of professional supervision. These are technical skills, administrative skills, and interpersonal skills.

Element 1: Technical Skills

Many business schools have for decades touted the idea that good managers can manage anything, moving from organization to organization and using their managerial skills equally well wherever they go. While there are many instances where general managers have transferred successfully from one company to another, there is a growing number of cases where the successful president of firm A falls apart and gets sacked on moving to the presidency of firm B. It is increasingly apparent that supervisors need some solid grounding in the technology of the business which they are directing as front-line management.

Being a project manager in a computer firm calls for a thorough knowledge of computers. An engineering degree is essential for an engineering project director so that the engineers working on the project will respond to his or her leadership. In other high-tech businesses a similar level of technological know-how is required for first-line supervisory success.

As a rule of thumb, the more complex the technology, and the faster it changes, the more valuable a college degree in the underlying discipline becomes. The supervisor must be able to keep abreast of technical changes in the product and processes.

In some businesses it is a matter of organizational culture that only a college-trained professional can hold a first-level management job. DuPont, for example, always insists that its supervisors have a chemical engineering degree or a background in chemistry.

Where the business is low in technology and high in common sense, a college degree may not be necessary. Experience and on-the-job training in the technical aspects of the work can take the place of a degree. For assembly-line supervision, for example, a hands-on knowledge of operations is all that is needed from a technical viewpoint in most organizations, and this is gained from experience.

Technological updating of first-line supervisors is a current need. Few firms do such training now. Rather, they leave it to their supervisors to retrain themselves on their own.

Element 2: Administrative Skills

Technical skills alone are insufficient for effective supervisory performance. Too often the technically trained person becomes trapped by details of technical work, leaving administrative chores undone or incompetently done. These include such matters as making sure that the work is rationally divided among all subordinates, that objectives are being attained, that all legal and policy requirements are understood and complied with, that reports and controls are skillfully applied, that quality is up to standard, and that cost constraints are adhered to.

Supervisors have three primary administrative responsibilities:

1. A system of management by objectives is the basic administrative building block for all supervisors—line and staff, production and service, business and nonprofit organization alike. At the start of every year the supervisor should systematically hold a formal discussion with every employee on the responsibilities of his or her job and on the standards of performance in each area of responsibility. These objectives then become the criteria for judging performance, improving it, and training people to improve their work.

2. A system of management by anticipation is needed by supervisors for mapping out what regular things need doing, what major problems should be tackled, and where improvements are

needed. Planning work fully is part of the administrative job of the supervisor, as is seeing, anticipating, and preventing problems. Supervisors should be looking for long-range as well as short-range plans for improvement of their departments or projects.

3. Maintaining managerial control is another key administrative responsibility for supervisors. The grandest objectives and strategies are pointless and futile unless they are executed well, and it's the first-line supervisor who is the key to execution. Once mapped out, plans, goals, standards of performance, and tolerances comprise the basis for reviewing actual performance. This requires daily supervision for checking and correcting while the work is going on. Periodic review of results against goals involves talking to people about their results. Personal inspection is a characteristic of the supervisory job, though not of higher executive level posts. The old adage for bridge players, "One peek is worth two finesses," suits the administrative role of a supervisor quite well.

In addition to these primary administrative responsibilities, other parts of the tool kit of the skilled supervisor include use of cost accounting, systems design, and systems management.

Element 3: Interpersonal Skills

Numerous studies of why supervisors get fired reveal that most such separations result from a lack of interpersonal skills, not from any lack of technical or administrative skills. Joseph Juran studied why a number of quality control supervisors got sacked and found that almost none were dismissed for technical shortcomings. Similar studies among fired accounting and engineering supervisors showed similar results. Behavioral shortcomings were cited as the reason almost all of the people studied were fired. They were too rough and tough or too easygoing, or they didn't relate well to customers, their bosses, or other supervisors.

I believe there are three basic interpersonal skills which first-line supervisors must have to succeed today:

1. *A basic understanding of human behavior*—knowing people's basic needs, wants, values, aspirations, and motivations, and how they adapt to change. Most workers today have middle-class

values; few have the mind-set of the uneducated or powerless worker. Women, minorities, older workers, and handicapped people are in the work force in ever greater numbers, and working with each of these groups requires special kinds of understanding. Continual training in this area is a minimum strategy for the organization which would keep its supervisors abreast of the times.

2. *Communications skills*—listening, talking, writing, conducting effective conferences of various types, and knowledge of organizational communications systems. Skill in conducting face-to-face discussions and such things as transactional analysis, negotiations, team building, and effective use of communications media are part of this battery of tools. For staff supervisors, writing is often a key to successful performance. This is needed for reports, letters, position papers, and the like.

3. *Values clarification* is a third key area of interpersonal skills for the professional supervisor. Failing to respect the values of people of both sexes and of all ages, races, and ethnic backgrounds will lead to serious problems for the organization in terms of job performance as well as in labor relations and in meeting the requirements of Equal Employment Opportunity laws.

Some supervisors see the values of people as enemies to be destroyed, and see the people themselves as tools to be employed and exploited. This is the Theory X supervisor. The Theory Y supervisor, on the other hand, sees people as having a capacity to be bigger, better, smarter, and maybe even nobler than they presently are. This Theory Y person sees the job of supervision as that of discovering—and realizing—the potential of his or her subordinates.

3
Getting New Employees Aboard and Integrated

Moreover thou shalt provide out of all the people able men, such as fear God, men of truth, hating covetousness; and place such over them, to be rulers of thousands, and rulers of hundreds, rulers of fifties, and rulers of tens.

—Exodus 18:21

Perhaps the most chronic problem facing management is the staffing of their organization with able people at all levels. Philip Marvin catalogs the reasons why organizations need new talent at one time or another: Organization growth demands new positions be filled; present employees are hired away; people die or their health fails and they can't perform any more; we neglect to develop the potential of our present people; competition upgrades its organization and we must rise to that challenge with new people; and finally, people fail to perform and must lamentably be replaced, hopefully with others who can.

Organizations such as IBM which grow in multibillion-dollar yearly increments require a steady stream of qualified new people to be infused at the bottom. Exxon, in the face of an oil surplus in 1986, stated that it would offer early retirement to up to 25 percent of its staff. If economic prosperity returns to the firm their needs for new people will be astronomical.

The business press reports regularly how one large firm or another hired a new president after a national search, only to let the winner go after a short stint in the new position. Even at the highest levels of government the process for selecting senior executives is a "hidden tragedy," according to one long-time senior official.

All of these and many more cases make it clear that hiring people is a chronic concern and one which has been widely studied.

Hugo Munsterberg of Harvard experimented in 1914 with the use
of tests for the scientific selection of personnel. In World War I the
Army's Committee on Classification of Personnel used testing to
assign inductees. Libraries are replete with texts on the employment
process. That this problem has been attacked by many and solved
adequately by few is evidenced by the chronic search for better employment methods. Despite the failures and conflicting testimony
about the best system of hiring new managers, there are some generally accepted principles and systems now in use.

Most such systems agree that the first stage of hiring is to define
in considerable detail the position to be filled. For some this consists
of a general definition of the personal and job requirements. Such
expressions as "Must be a thinker and a doer; college degree pre-
ferred" are typical of job advertisements. Detailed job descriptions
are widely used as a basis for screening applicants. Prospecting
widely for candidates is generally agreed to be useful; the more options considered, the better the choice. An intensive study of the life
and work history of the applicants is another principle which is
considered to be sound practice, along with interviewing and ref-
erence checking. For some, testing is proposed. These procedures
have been described in a systematic form in Philip Matheny's book
Critical Path Hiring. Beyond these commonly accepted procedures,
there are some further practices which can improve the hiring
decision.

Nine Rules for Hiring New Employees

To avoid hiring the wrong people, you need to think about staffing
needs over a longer term than simply getting next week's or next
month's job done. Your best bet is to think of employees as part of
an investment portfolio—your human resources portfolio. The high
costs of hiring are only a small part of the total bill, for the salaries
you pay in the years ahead will be higher than ever and the effects
of poor performance will outweigh acquisition and salary costs by
a wide margin.

Constructing a human resources portfolio calls for thinking in
two dimensions for every person you hire: first, the performance
level expected on the present job, and second, the potential of the

individual for doing bigger and better jobs in the future. In hiring an eighteen-year-old messenger today, you may also be hiring a clerk five years from now. In hiring a new machinist, you might also be hiring a master mechanic or machine shop supervisor ten years from now. By considering both dimensions when first hiring an employee, you can avoid being stuck with deadwood or a problem child ten years down the road.

There are a number of rules which an objective investment counselor will give to an individual investor which you can easily convert from buying stocks and bonds to buying people for your organization's future. If you think about the people you hire as additions to your portfolio of assets, here are nine proven rules which you should tack on your wall during the coming year when your organization may be hiring new employees.

Rule 1: Diversify Your Portfolio

In an investment portfolio, don't bet all your funds on blue-chip stocks but get a mix to cover a variety of possibilities in the future. In human resources as well, variety is the key to a sound portfolio. Don't select people who all fit the same mold. Choose some stars along with the workhorses, and maybe even a hard-to-manage type if he or she has great potential. Mix experienced and inexperienced, and people of a wide variety of ages. Don't hire all young people or all old-timers. To avoid serious legal problems in the future, make sure that your mix includes some of the protected categories of employees, such as blacks, women, and people over the age of 45. Diversifying under the crunch of immediate job needs may seem a bit troublesome, but it will make for a better portfolio in the long pull.

Rule 2: Concentrate on Workhorses

Most of your human resources portfolio should consist of solid, reliable workhorses, with only a small complement of hotshots or stars. The college market is a buyer's market today and you may be tempted to load up on too many people who have a brilliant education rather than any real experience. But a mixture of a few stars with people who have solid experience (even though they may have less potential) will cover most situations better.

Rule 3: Avoid Mass Hiring

Don't try to fill every position you can imagine by bringing in too many people too fast. Shipyard experiences during World War II demonstrated the disastrous inefficiency which can follow when great bunches of people are hired all at once. Spread your hiring over as long a time span as possible and be more deliberate with each person you hire. Haste makes waste. Act like a smart investor, not a local draft board.

Rule 4: Buy Only What You Can Afford

Don't hire high-priced college graduates unless you are able to wait for their performance to come up to par. The smart investor knows that you don't buy common stocks unless you can afford to wait years for a payoff, especially in dealing with new issues. If you need an immediate payoff from your human resources investment, hire an experienced person. If you can afford it and want a longer "stream of income," then college grads may be a good investment. Just remember that it will probably take longer than you think to get the college grads up to their maximum stream of income for the firm.

Rule 5: Make Your Own Decisions

Don't buy a stock because it's a glamour issue that's being touted in the business press or by some stockbroker, and don't hire a person because he or she is being pushed by a headhunter, a consultant, or an employment agency. Don't rely on what somebody else says. If the job calls for business results, you need to look more closely at an individual's past job experience than at his or her reputation among outsiders.

In addition, it's a good idea to vary your sources of new employees. It often seems simple to get one good source and to have that source round up candidates for you, but that's a kind of laziness that could cost you dearly when the time comes for developing variety in your human resources portfolio. Don't hire from just the few colleges which *Fortune* and *Business Week* refer to as the leading business schools. Take a close look at each individual. The best people at the University of North Dakota are probably as good as the best people at some Ivy League school, though the bottom of each class may differ substantially.

Rule 6: Promote from Within

Hiring from outside is always a poor choice if, with a little more effort, you might have filled the job by promoting from within your organization. For one thing, direct hiring costs will be higher. For another, there are high hidden costs which will arise from lower morale and motivation among people who rightly conclude that opportunity for advancement is restricted. Thus it is best to hire from outside only for low-level positions. Middle-management and executive-level positions should be filled by promotion from within the organization. It is an admission of failure in training and development to hire outsiders who zoom into the upper ranks because no qualified person exists in the lower ranks of your own organization. There are, of course, exceptions to this rule in times of radical growth, but these don't obviate the principle.

Rule 7: Don't Play It Too Safe

Don't bet everything on low-price, low-risk, safe investments. Keep a certain percentage of your funds invested in issues which have a possibility of high gains even though they are attended by higher risks. Similarly, don't be afraid to take a chance on one or two high-potential employees. It may seem to be a high-risk venture for a small firm to hire an MBA for the first time, but the possibility of high gain is also present where it didn't exist before. In spite of Rule 6, the firm which has always found its managers from among people who worked their way up through the ranks should try the riskier but potentially highly rewarding move of hiring a star-quality younger performer. If you're careful, you may get a leavening influence in the organization that will raise the performance level of the rest of the people. Bringing a hotshot engineer from a top school into your engineering department may spur the rest of the people to new efforts and new performance that they wouldn't have achieved otherwise.

Remember that your investment portfolio mix is a function of your age, level of income, financial condition, and, above all, your financial objectives. Similarly, your human resources portfolio mix is a function of your organization's size, affluence, and, above all, your organizational objectives. If you are big, successful, and affluent, you can probably afford the risk of hiring an oddball who also happens to be highly talented in something which would be very useful to your organization.

Rule 8: Follow a Steady Course

Always hire more slowly than you think is necessary right after a recession. Once business starts pouring in the doors and the freeze on hiring is lifted, the temptation to start adding people left and right is almost irresistible, but it must be resisted. Oftentimes we are too slow in letting people go during the early stages of a downturn. Because we are human, we grow attached to people and are reluctant to chuck them out. But there is a corresponding tendency toward overhiring at the first clear signal that things are getting better. We tend to extrapolate today into next week and next year without the vaguest hint that things will ever stop going the way they are presently going. You need to avoid the sort of overhiring in good times which you will regret later on. Keep people working hard by running less fully staffed than you think is necessary. If you are proven wrong and the boom continues and people are getting really stressed, then add people as they are needed. Don't hire now to fill imaginary future needs.

Statistics show that labor costs decline in a recession as productivity increases, but that individual productivity declines when the recession ends and prosperity returns. What happens is that we often return to old habits of doing things when the times look better.

Rule 9: Don't Follow Somebody Else's System

There is no infallible system for beating the market. If there were such a system, those who knew it wouldn't be willing to share it because to do so would take away their advantage. Likewise, don't look for any infallible system for hiring the best people. The world is full of people making large sums in retainers and consultancy fees by assuring their clients that they have a foolproof system for finding the right person for every job. Their system may involve stress interviews, pattern interviews, biological screening, or lie detector tests. There are a variety of techniques that will enable you to do a better job in the hiring process, but your best bet is to try all of those which seem plausible and which have a good track record in your own organization (or in another organization whose success you admire).

The assessment of potential is the most difficult assessment to be made in the hiring process. A complete biographical history has been found to be the best predictor of what a person will do in the future. If the individual has been persistently successful in everything he or she has done in the past—as a kid, as a college student, and as an employee elsewhere—the chances are high that his or her success-seeking behavior will persist. The only hitch in this approach lies not in the person's background, which can be described either honestly or falsely, but in whether the successes of the past will carry over to the objectives of your organization in the future. A close check with past employers is clearly necessary to learn whether or not the behavior exhibited on the earlier jobs was successful for the employer.

Interviews, tests, biographical information, and a solid knowledge of the job objectives are the main ingredients in a good hiring system. No single system or gimmick presently exists which can produce the variety of answers which you need in hiring.

The first step in assembling a human resources portfolio is not to collect a list of candidates to interview. It's to carefully define the job objectives of the vacant position. Then you begin the process of screening people for those past behaviors which in all likelihood will indicate who best fits the objectives of the vacant position.

Your task is not one of identifying the personality traits of the ideal jobholder, nor one of describing the activities of the job. Defining job *objectives* is the starting place. Don't hire to fill a position without having those specific objectives clearly in mind. Though no one has a surefire way to hire only winners, you can raise your chances of success in constructing a solid portfolio—of investments or people—by following these nine rules and starting with a knowledge of your objectives.

Seventeen Guides for Performance Appraisal

More than 25 years ago Douglas McGregor wrote a penetrating article entitled "An Uneasy Look at Performance Review" in which he pointed out the damaging effects that a bad performance review can have upon subordinate performance. Then, in quite sweeping terms, he proposed that some major new approaches were required, concluding that management by objectives provided the best basis for measuring managerial performance.

Robert Lefton, a principal in Psychological Associates of St. Louis, reports that the flaws McGregor found are still present. In a study he conducted in 1984, 70 percent of the 4,000 employees in 190 firms reported that their boss didn't give them a clear picture of what's expected of them, and only 20 percent said that their performance on results was reviewed.

This and other evidence makes it clear that many managers still have trouble with reviewing the performance of their subordinates. The following seventeen guides to conducting successful performance reviews should prove useful for all managers:

1. *Review the performance of every employee periodically.* The pressures of day-to-day operations often make the conduct of annual performance reviews a matter of low priority for many bosses. Yet people are not motivated when they don't know how well they are doing in their work. People need to know what is expected of them, and they need to know how well—or poorly—they have done. Performance appraisal is a basic part of every manager's job, but it's often poorly done or not done at all. Performance review is a serious matter, with long-term implications for the human resource development of the organization.

2. *Develop an organization-wide review system.* If specific units are allowed to remain out of the system, or to use individually designed formats, inequity is bound to appear. The basic assumptions behind the appraisal plans used by various managers in an organization must be identical, as well as the standards and methods of measurement. A common format should be developed for use by all managers. Without such a system, or with too-frequent changes in the system, the inventory of human resources will become blurred over time and many of the qualities of the organization's people will be unknown. Human resources are too crucial an asset not to be assessed by some common standards.

3. *Obtain top management acceptance.* While staff experts in management development play an important role in designing the system, this is too vital a task to be left solely to them. The details of the appraisal plan and methods of performance review need the wholehearted acceptance of senior officers, division managers, and major department heads. This sort of acceptance by line management enhances the likelihood that the system will be used. Simplicity in operation is ordinarily one of their major requirements.

4. *Train every manager in how to conduct a performance review.* Court decisions in discrimination cases have sometimes hinged on whether or not the performance review system was consistently applied. In some cases the judge has concluded that a lack of training in how the system should operate is evidence that the system could not be consistently applied. Judges and courts aside, when you have a system designed to implement a performance review policy, it makes good sense to provide adequate training to those who must make the system function well. Hence you should get your trainers moving on providing soundly constructed and effective mandatory training for all managers. Too many performance review programs have been undertaken with just the distribution of a review form and a lengthy cover letter. Classroom training with role-playing exercises and discussion is essential.

5. *Conduct objectives-centered performance reviews.* The choice of standards or yardsticks against which the review will take place should be centered around the job objectives of the individual whose performance is being reviewed. Subjectivity, which is inherent in personality-based reviews, only invites trouble. People don't want to have their personalities treated as company property, but

they are eager to learn how well they have done in accomplishing the objectives of their job. For objectives-centered reviews to work, a boss and subordinate must first sit down and negotiate job objectives for the coming period. Then, with such objectives clarified and confirmed in writing, the standards of performance to be used in the annual review are clear, useful, and productive. No other standards work as well.

6. *Conduct reviews both periodically and continuously.* It is essential to sit down for a planned discussion of results and future objectives once a year, but this isn't the whole job of performance review. Each manager must also assume responsibility for providing continuous feedback of results to each subordinate throughout the year. Timely information about how well one is doing in one's work is an absolute necessity if people are to grow. The annual review is a summary of all the little bits of recognition which have piled up during the year. When added to these continuous reviews, the annual review contains no surprises for the subordinate.

There is a chance that too much feedback could turn into a form of nagging or overly close supervision. Thus, continuous review works best when people have clearly defined job objectives, as well as a means of measuring their own performance on the job while they are doing it.

7. *Plan your performance reviews carefully.* Both bosses and subordinates should be required to do advance planning for the periodic performance review. The superior collects the objectives agreed upon in advance and evidence of the actual results achieved, and also puts together an agenda of selected topics for the subordinate's development. The subordinate in turn should be asked to prepare for the review by considering both the original objectives and the results attained. The subordinate should also be invited to bring to the review any other concerns which are on his or her mind.

8. *Schedule individual sessions carefully.* Get out your date book and schedule every person who works for you to come in for their annual review. Don't let anything cause you to miss anybody. Winter vacations, scheduled travel, or special urgent projects are often used as an excuse by people who would like to finesse the whole thing. Make it clear that everybody gets to come in, even if you have to do it after hours on your own time.

9. *Center the discussion on goals and results.* "These are the goals you set; now let's look at how the results came out" is an excellent starting point. Avoid casting blame, finding fault, or turning the performance review into a hell-raising session. Don't focus upon personal strengths and weaknesses, nor on personality and character. Stick to the goals and results. If the subordinate seems to be trying to get you to criticize his or her personality, shift the subject. Some people would love to have you discuss their character in general terms in order to direct the spotlight away from their performance failures.

10. *Take as much time as necessary.* You will find that many performance review sessions will extend beyond the time you had planned for them. When this happens, schedule another appointment to continue the discussion in the near future. Often you will be engaging in some hard bargaining about goals and resolving some disagreements about what should be done and how it should be done, and that takes a lot of time. If the subordinate has something to discuss, listen fully and restate what has been said to indicate that you understand it and how the person apparently feels about it. You don't have to agree or disagree, just hear the person out fully. In doing this you show that you care about the other person and his or her opinions. If you interrupt or make judgments you stifle further dialogue and miss out on a lot of valuable information.

11. *Do more listening than talking.* If you start a monologue and deliver a lecture during the performance review, you'll miss out on the contribution that the subordinate can make. You will also stifle the other person's independence and creativity and probably lose a substantial part of the benefit that can be obtained from the performance review. Ask a lot of questions to clarify what has been said. If the subordinate arrives at some insight, restate it. Keep the focus of the session on the other person, not on you or your problems. Active listening requires full attention, so don't be doing paperwork on the side or taking phone calls during the session. Make it clear that you consider this conference to be extremely important.

12. *Seek consensus.* Get the subordinate to arrive at some kind of summary about his or her performance. If the person is patently missing something important, ask questions to get at the facts. Lis-

ten carefully for evidence that the other person sees the real nature of the problem and intends to do something constructive, then summarize that understanding. Don't be too exacting or judgmental, but don't agree to things you can't accept either.

13. *Focus on the future, not the past.* The purpose of performance review is not simply to go over the past and find out what went wrong and why. Rather, it should review the past to find opportunities for future successes. The key question isn't "Why did you fail?" but "How can we sew that up so we don't get caught again?" or "How could you do an even better job next year?" Ask for ideas on how the subordinate can improve his or her performance in terms of quantity, quality, cost, service, and time. Forward-looking questions are positive in tone and show promise for a better future. An emphasis on past failures doesn't improve things, but it does dampen enthusiasm and reduce motivation.

14. *Make notes during the discussion.* Having scheduled all your team members for review sessions within a relatively short time span, you can't remember everything that is said. It's a good idea to make notes while the other person is talking. List the highlights of the discussion. People aren't usually offended by this, and some are flattered that their boss is interested enough in what they have to say to make notes. Then use your notes to give a summary at the end of the session. If the other person doesn't agree with your summary, accept the correction, especially to any errors in fact. Use the notes as a tool to make sure that you have listened, not as a rope to hang somebody.

15. *Ask supportive questions.* One of the best ways to indicate that you are supportive and caring is to ask three questions of the subordinate near the end of the discussion: (a) What can I do to help you do an even better job? (b) What could I do differently to help? (c) Is there anything I can refrain from doing to make it easier for you to do your job? Listen to what the subordinate says, then deliver on those things which are possible for you to do. If you can't deliver on some of them, say so. Rensis Likert's research demonstrates that supportive bosses have the best relationships with their subordinates, and that subordinates who work for supportive bosses have the highest levels of motivation.

16. *Confirm agreements in writing.* When the review is com-

pleted, confirm in writing all agreements which have been made. Make it clear that the first draft is subject to revisions in the event that you have misstated anything. And make it clear that the agreements are commitments for the future and that both parties are in substantial agreement on the conclusions concerning the subordinate's performance. Prepare a Performance Notebook with separate pockets for each subordinate. During the period before the next review, slip information into the notebook about results, special accomplishments, training, changes and modifications in goals, and the addition of new targets of opportunity which have been agreed upon. Make this a living document, not one that's cast in concrete. If conditions change and the goals need changing, don't fail to call for an amendment session. Talk the changes out fully and confirm the amendment in writing, then file this in your notebook with the original goals memo.

17. *Build self-esteem and increase motivation.* The objective of the performance review is to improve performance, which can be done by building self-esteem and increasing the motivation of employees. Don't allow yourself to play judge and jury. Indicate openly that you want people to succeed, that you support their efforts, and that you stand ready to help. Make it a "we" discussion rather than a "you" discussion. Cover all aspects of the job and performance, not just the failures. Don't hesitate to let people know that you have confidence in them and that you hold them in high regard as individuals even when they have occasionally failed to achieve what they set out to do. Also let them know that you expect them to keep growing and progressing in their work and career. Discuss personal development goals along with job objectives, and suggest new ways for them to develop professionally and personally.

4
The Role of Style
in Building Integration

Truth has given way to credibility, facts to statements that sound authoritative without conveying any authoritative information . . . .
—Christopher Lasch

In the investment management community, one of the elements which determines the prospects of a company stock for investors is the managerial style of the top people. Some managers' styles are labeled as "lean and mean," which usually evokes a wave of murmured admiration among the portfolio managers. It is presumed that such a style will produce tough decisions to cut costs without sentimentality or excessive concern for such things as love, loyalty to employees, or hate. The lean-and-mean manager is one who will coldly close a plant if it proves to be a loser, regardless of the impact upon the community or the long-service employees. This management style will keep its eye on short-term profit. Such profits are imperative for the portfolio manager, since a single quarter of lackluster performance in profit and sales growth will produce a drop in stock prices and hence the value of the portfolio. Multiyear perspectives for deferred growth and earnings can be safely ignored in such a climate.

For the chief executive of the publicly owned firm, this array of investor judges often dominates his manner of managing the organization. Division managers are hired and fired according to their ability to produce an ever-increasing stream of earning, quarter after quarter. Knowing this, the division manager resorts to management-by-pressure of subordinates in manufacturing, sales, and engineering. This in turn converts into supervisory pressures on the work force. As one supervisor told me: "The big wheel makes a quarter turn, and smaller wheels make a hundred revolutions."

The sense of powerlessness which permeates the pressure-driven organization grows proportionately as pressure from the top increases at lower levels. The portfolio manager is interested in the value of his or her holdings, not out of greed but out of stewardship of the pension trusts and mutual funds being managed. This goal is perhaps understandable and even proper, for who would want their retirement income jeopardized by managers who are uneasy about cutting waste and unnecessary costs? The effect, however, can be an organization where the hardened management style erodes employee trust and confidence in the future.

Less noble than the protection of the income of widows, orphans, and pensioners, however, are the pressures which come from speculators and arbitragers who use the mechanics of corporate finance to exert ungodly pressures on even the best run and most stable and profitable organizations. Recent arrests of a ring of young arbitragers, investment analysts and brokers who were playing games with the world of corporate finance through insider trading, is a less palatable explanation of the pressure on management to become lean and mean.

How Management Style Affects Integration and Self-Control

There are endless taxonomies and laundry lists of the kinds of style which managers might adopt and pursue as their own. In one widely noted list, Michael Maccoby classified them into four categories. The prevailing style today, he suggests, is the *gamesman,* a flexible, competitive player, a glory seeker. Other managers, less likely to rise, are the *craftsmen,* who base their self-worth on knowledge, skill, discipline, and self-reliance. Such persons, says Maccoby, are on the defensive, trying to protect their integrity from the exploitative demands of the more aggressive managerial types. A third style is that of the *jungle fighter,* who has been traditionally an entrepreneur and empire builder. Such types don't shrink from using force, guile, and domination to achieve their grandiose ends. People are objects to be used. Jungle fighters generally mistrust their own subordinates, considering them to be lazy, stupid, and probably a bit dishonest. The fourth category, which, Maccoby declares, describes the middle-management ranks of most bureaucratic organizations, is the *company man* who has sold his independence, individualism, and self-reliance for a steady position and predictable income. For such people the differences between themselves and the organization are thin if not indistinguishable. Because the company man lacks the risk-taking ability, confidence, toughness, self-control, and energy to reach the top, he enforces conformity upon all those below him in rank.

Many firms today are reported to be seeking a more entrepreneurial type of manager, especially for general management roles in start-up and growth lines of products and business. Combining the qualities of the company man and the jungle fighter who will work within the framework of General Electric, General Motors, or 3M, they are called *intrapreneurs*. They work for a paycheck and perhaps a bonus if they succeed, but are just lacking in enough jungle-fighter qualities to quit the large firm and launch out on their own.

Clearly the choice of a management style is difficult today, for the pressures from outside the company pull and push the rising manager in several diametrically opposed directions. The choice of a style usually isn't as much an individual decision as a result of systems pressures. The manager who chooses to be an integrator must operate in such a way that his reliance upon subordinates doesn't compromise his own effectiveness and efficiency in achieving the tasks which are his responsibility.

Balance in Management

This self-controlled organization which desires to integrate the best talents of its work force with the demands of the company must walk a fine line. It calls for what consultant Clark Caskey terms "balance in management." What is to be balanced? One must avoid falling into the trap of being so tough, lean-and-mean, and confrontational that he alienates the very people whose performance is needed to produce the results demanded by the investors and top management. At the other extreme, one must avoid toppling into the game of operating a firm for the exclusive purpose of making all of the employees happy.

This balance is expressed by Robert Blake in his book *Mana-*

gerial Grid as the extremes of operating a sweatshop as opposed to heading a country club. This leaves the manager in a position where he must combine two apparently conflicting goals into a productive, unified, and satisfying organization for workers and investors. Blake rates this as a 9.9 manager, one who maintains equal pressure for productivity and for concern for the workers' values and needs.

Since fence-walking requires mainly that one not fall on one side or the other, it comes out as a balancing act between the pitfalls of destroying the trust of workers and, on the other side, avoiding confrontation with unpleasant truths and situations. Let's look at these two sides and how to avoid being toppled too far in either direction.

Building Trust Calls for Predictable Behavior

Although a lot has been written about choosing a management style, little attention has been paid to the element of trust. Yet if subordinates have a high level of trust in management, they can readily adapt to the unique hardness or softness in the personal manners of the boss. But if they don't trust management, the style of the individual manager isn't especially important either. That is, if you can rely upon your boss to behave in a consistent and predictable way, you can modify your own behavior.

It's far easier to work for a boss whose behavior is predictable, even if the predictable boss is a hard-nosed screamer while the unpredictable one is generally jolly and warm. When the behavior of the boss is unpredictable, mistrust dominates the boss/subordinate relationship.

Some historians even attribute the American Revolution to the inconsistent behavior of King George III and the English parliament rather than to harsh and unfair taxes and tariffs. There's an important moral in this, for it illustrates how managers can erode the trust of their subordinates in the managers' right and authority to rule. This is sometimes a matter of moods, but even if the boss is prone to blow his or her cool occasionally, people can learn how to adapt to such outbursts when the storms come at predictable times or for predictable causes.

Managerial Bait-and-Switch Games

One of the most detested scams in the world of commerce is the bait-and-switch tactic used by a few shady merchants in their advertising. They place a large display ad in the newspaper offering something at a fantastically low price, but when you get to the store you learn that the advertised goods are sold out and you are offered something that's "just as good" at twice the price. This tactic becomes outright fraud when they try to sell something shoddy while pretending it's the real thing, or when they sell you one thing and then deliver an inferior substitute. Consumer protection laws were written in large part to protect unwary buyers from such bait-and-switch maneuvers. But bait-and-switch games are also a part of the managerial practices of both business and nonprofit organizations, according to a number of interviews which I've conducted with victims.

My own first contact with a supervisory example of bait-and-switch occurred when I was eighteen years old and landed a job stacking tin cans into a boxcar at a New Jersey factory. The foreman, an oily-smiling weasel, showed me how to fork cans from a fast-running production line into freight cars. I worked at a herculean level to keep ahead of the line on the first morning, convinced that I would die of exhaustion before noon. I collapsed and rested during the lunch hour. When the line started up again, I picked up my stacking fork and made ready to try to keep ahead of this Niagara-like flow for the rest of the day. Suddenly a more senior manager appeared and asked, "Where's the second stacker?" I stared in disbelief. "You mean that this is a job for two men?" I replied while dropping the stacking fork. That rascally foreman had decided to save the company some money by seeing if I could handle double the workload of any ordinary worker all by myself!

This, I have come to learn, is a common managerial variation of the bait-and-switch game. First you hire someone to do a job, then you pile on an ungodly amount of extra work when the new person comes aboard. If the gullible novice does it, you simply treat that as the standard for the job. Labor history is filled with examples of this practice. Miners who were promised an ordinary miner's job would find that the output standards were hiked to virtually impossible levels by the boss, and then treated as the new standard. When unions came along promising to police "a fair day's work for a fair day's pay" they were welcomed with open arms. Thereafter, of course, the unions worked diligently to get as little work for the most pay possible to offset bait-and-switch work standards of the past.

The point here isn't that such practices are still allowed in well-run manufacturing operations. It's that bait-and-switch is more likely to be worked today on technical, professional, and managerial people by their superiors. Several national surveys reveal that the level of trust in top management by mid- and lower-level managers was never worse. Much of that low level of trust has been created, I would suggest, by the widespread practice of bait-and-switch management.

As I mentioned earlier, the business press frequently carries reports of how some new chief executive gets hired by a large corporation and then either quits or is fired within a few months. But in following up with the victims of several such events, I found that the rotation often occurred because the boss had pulled a bait-and-switch on the newly hired executive.

Take the case of a large East Coast consumer goods corporation in which the aging founder, at the urging of the board, had finally consented to hire a successor. He conducted a national search and hired an impressive star away from another firm amid congratulations and sighs of relief that a qualified successor was now in place. But then he kept tossing new and impossible objectives to the new man which had not been discussed during the hiring interviews. Some of them had even been specifically denied as being a part of the job. A showdown soon came and an acrimonious separation resulted.

"Our understanding was that I was to become president and chief operating officer, with full responsibility for all aspects of operations," one short-term executive told me. "But after I arrived I learned that the job description had been doctored and now I was expected to be manager of three divisions which were without general managers, in addition to being the chief operating officer of the whole firm with responsibility over seven other division managers who were reporting to me. I found myself spending most of my time doing work I never signed up for, and when I pressed the chief to get on with approving replacements for the three vacant division manager positions he simply smiled and suggested we stick with the present arrangement for a while longer. After six months I found a better job and quit."

Even if a bait-and-switch maneuver isn't deliberately or maliciously executed, the effect is the same as if it were.

Distinguishing between Stings and Challenges

Unlike professional con men whose business and pleasure is in singling out and victimizing a mark (usually by taking the person's life savings), the managerial bait-and-switch game is usually played by people in high places with the best of motives. They simply want to increase efficiency and think that increasing the responsibility of their subordinates is a challenge which will help them realize their full potential. So far, so good. But challenges are different from sting operations.

The moment which con men call the sting occurs when the victim realizes that he or she has been taken in. Once stung, you become a wiser person and less likely to be disappointed in future deals, and also less likely to trust people. On the other hand, a "challenge" comes when you take on a tough assignment with your eyes open and then discover that it is even worse than you imagined. You then have to rev up your engine and work harder and smarter than you realized was possible.

Lee Iacocca knew that Chrysler was in trouble when he took over, but, as he reports in his autobiography, the situation proved to be far worse than he had imagined. This wasn't a sting, however; nobody had promised him a serene berth on a cruise ship in calm seas. Had Gene Cafiero and the board papered over information to assure him that everything was great and then thrown him to the wolves, that would have been a sting.

Employers know that they have to guard against job applicants who oversell their credentials or experience in a form of bait-and-switch, but the applicants often aren't alert to the fact that employers may victimize them in the same game. Deliberately concealing the scope of a job is a bait-and-switch maneuver at which some people have considerable skill.

When companies reorganize to increase their efficiency it usually means that duties will be combined. Maybe a whole layer of management will be eliminated, leaving more work for those kept on board. This is a natural environment for the skilled bait-and-switch executives to work a scam on the people who are shuffled to new positions. A hiring freeze may be a sensible tightening of an organization to eliminate fat, or it could be a bait-and-switch tactic.

In one large organization where labor relations had fallen into disarray, a divisional industrial-relations manager was elevated to the top corporate job. Nothing was said about cutting his staff, but when he arrived in his new job he discovered that he had no lawyers or analysts to implement vital research and strategic bargaining practices. He ended up doing a lot of dog-work on his own. Within a year he parlayed his experience into a vice presidency in another firm, where he reported confidentially that he had been "sandbagged by top management" in his old job.

The U.S. Congress pulled a bait-and-switch on the federal civil service senior executives in 1979. First they passed legislation to pay bonuses on top of the regular pay for setting and achieving objectives, then they refused to appropriate money to pay the promised bonuses. When asked to justify his position on this reneging, one congressman stated curtly, "Congress has the power."

How to Avoid Being Stung

There are six ways you can avoid being trapped in a bait-and-switch management system:

1. As much as you can, negotiate the conditions for which you are to be held responsible in your job. A well-planned and well-executed MBO system is solid insurance against bait-and-switch.

2. Confirm in writing the agreements you make with your boss about your responsibilities. Do your hard bargaining before the year begins, not after you've started or at the end of the period.

3. Ask specific questions about what is expected. Get all the bad news up front. What are my major areas of responsibility?

What results will be expected? What resources will be available for me to do the job? How much freedom will I have and what kinds of controls must I respond to? What policies might affect my job performance? What is my authority to spend money, hire and fire personnel, and initiate independent action? The idea is to establish "management by contract" to assure that every manager knows in advance what to expect.

4. Know the constraints and limitations you face, as well as who makes what decisions. You won't be victimized, for example, if your boss holds onto the decision-making power for expenditures in excess of $10,000. You may not like it, but at least you know where you stand.

5. Rate your own performance while you are performing. If you have enough information about objectives, standards, constraints, and the resources available to you, you can usually tell how well you are doing in your work while you are doing it. Thus you can use self-control to step up your own levels of energy or to redirect your efforts along more productive lines.

6. Schedule quarterly reviews with your boss to talk about your progress, knock out inappropriate goals, and add new targets as opportunities come along. If external conditions change, for example, it may be necessary to establish new output levels or to change your objectives.

Three months into the operating year, one large firm ordered a 20 percent budget cut. Every manager had to comply and none of them liked it, but it wasn't an act of bad faith. In another firm, however, overhead charges were recalculated in the tenth month of an otherwise successful year, thus adding substantially to the costs charged against various units without allowing for any change in objectives. In this instance, managers quite justifiably felt that they had been victimized by a bait-and-switch version of MBO.

Build Trust with Honesty

We can't always avoid being caught in a managerial bait-and-switch and, when it is done to us we may be forced to do it to those who work for us. If you find that you must break some promises you've made to your subordinates, it's best to explain fully what has happened and to assure them that you are supportive and understanding of their disappointment or anger.

Unless you can assure your people that they can rely upon you and that your behavior will be consistent, you'll see good people leaving for better working conditions and the least valuable people staying to play games of "cover your anatomy." Without trust, commitment will decline, risk taking and innovation will dry up, your MBO system will falter even though people continue to go through the motions, and you can scratch any idea you had of becoming an organization characterized by managerial excellence.

Is Tough-minded Confrontation Suitable for the Eighties?

There are, without doubt, plenty of advantages in using the behavioral sciences in management. Skills in motivation, building teams, and getting participation are well taught in most management training courses. The age of the roughneck or tough guy in management appears to be well on the road to oblivion.

In humanizing work we have done some good things for the quality of work life. We have, for example, made it unacceptable behavior for managers to kick people around. People at work today, especially the well-educated professionals and technicians who are a significant portion of the work force, simply won't accept hard-nosed management techniques. Management by fear is simply not allowed in most major corporations these days.

Nevertheless we'd be misinterpreting the new rules of conduct if we were to presume that managers no longer engage in confrontations. The plain fact is that managers must often confront situations, people, and wrongheaded behavior without flinching and without backing down. The art of being tough-minded without being tough-hearted or tough-talking is one of the skills which experience and training can bring to managers.

One of the basic rules that bosses must learn is that the inability to face problems when they crop up won't win them any permanent medals from their subordinates. Bosses who try to push problems under the rug or who pretend that they don't exist usually don't

earn the respect they seek. Douglas McGregor once charged that modern managers too often don't face reality in their organizations. They bury themselves in figures, charts, financial data, and statistics rather than look at the organization as a human structure. When this occurs, he said, they remove themselves and the decisions from reality, and the quality of their decisions is steadily eroded.

Take the case of the boss who sees a subordinate regularly failing to achieve his or her objectives but who doesn't feel that it's important enough to tell the person exactly how he or she is failing. The entire process of goal setting gets watered down quickly in such an environment, because performance will slip when people learn that they aren't going to be held accountable for their results.

Failing to face up to incompetence, insubordination, slipshod work, bad work habits, or laxity in living up to company policies can make all of these things acceptable to an ever-increasing number of subordinates. The foreman who sees a worker not using goggles in defiance of the safety rules is inviting accidents. So the offender is a strong-willed person who loves to stick his or her tongue out at the rules? That doesn't make the rules any less meaningful, nor does it make the required action any less important to implement. It merely means that the manager isn't doing the job the way it should be done if he or she ignores the safety rule violation. Similarly the middle- or upper-level manager who insists upon cutting corners on important rules and policies is also in need of being confronted by his or her boss.

Confrontation Calls for Progressive Discipline

The purpose of discipline is the same for a division manager who ignores corporate policies as for a worker who violates safety rules. There are certain kinds of behavior which are unacceptable and which must be corrected.

Take the case of a division manager who decided that a corporate policy against competing with customers was nonsense and who seized on a period of internal unrest in his firm's top management to go after forbidden business. The strategy of the firm was to sell only to original-equipment manufacturers. The manager

thought he could make an end run around his customers by marketing replacement parts to his customers' customers. However, the
regional equipment manufacturers who comprised the major market for the firm's product began to change suppliers, and the business slipped badly. The lesson is clear: A manager who doesn't like
a particular policy has the right—even an obligation—to carry his
or her arguments upstairs and to try to persuade people up there
that their policy is wrong-headed or even foolish. But if the decision
is made to stick with the policy, then the manager who deviates
from it should be brought up short and confronted with his or her
rebelliousness.

President Harry Truman established this principle in his confrontation with General Douglas MacArthur. MacArthur was convinced that the policy of not carrying the war to China was both
militarily and diplomatically wrong, and he made his opinion clear
to his superiors in Washington. Given explicit orders to avoid such
an enlargement of the Korean war, the general nonetheless carried
the battle to the Yalu, with some rather disastrous results. The general chose to place his own views over those of his legitimate boss.
Truman, no stranger to confrontation in his many years of politics,
didn't flinch. He fired a national hero and underwent all kinds of
hell from the press, his political opponents, and the congress. Time,
however, seems to indicate that he behaved properly. Maybe a lesser
leader could learn from Truman.

Listen carefully to every subordinate opinion, but once a decision is made, hold people accountable for staying within the given
policies. Harold Geneen, president of ITT during its great growth
years, relied upon three laws which he applied to his subordinates:

1. All decisions should be fact-based. This says, in effect, "If I
   can't trust your facts, don't ask me to accept your opinion."

2. All important decisions affecting subordinates should be
   made face-to-face. You can do a better job of judging the
   truth in a situation when you are looking the other person in
   the eye.

3. All problems are to be reported to the next highest level before they become impossible to solve.

Fact-based decisions require a managerial style in which managers are willing to confront unpleasant facts as readily as the pleasing and happy news.

Facts are not biases, hunches, or intuitions, although subordinates may try to pass these off to you as facts. A fact is a condition for which there is a preponderance of favorable evidence, not a widely held opinion. Good questions and good listening are part of the manager's tool kit for digging out facts.

Confront Long-Range Prospects

It is necessary to confront long-range prospects as well as the immediate problem. When R.J. Reynolds was presented with a market threat by the surgeon general's declaration that its major product—cigarettes—causes lung cancer, it adopted a new strategy for growth by launching an orderly movement into other businesses, including liquor, food, shipping, and theme parks. Eleven years after the potentially disastrous revelations of the surgeon general, it has proved the value of confronting hard facts with strategic change.

US Steel stands on the verge of being a non-steel business today. It was confronted with foreign competition which it saw few real opportunities for beating. By acquiring energy businesses, purchasing steel from England for sale in the U.S., and developing strategies aimed at survival as a business, though not as a steel company, US Steel exemplified how strategic confrontation works.

In personal career planning, as in business planning, confrontation with hard facts should lead us to new strategies. Factual evidence that one won't get to the high level aspired to is something that people have a hard time facing. Such a confrontation with one's own personal career situation is one of the hardest—and most important—we can make.

If you didn't do anything differently than you are doing right now, where will you be in five years and in ten years? What are some options open to you? Answering these questions is what self-confrontation in career management is all about. The immediate response may be to stay where you are, but you can start planning and preparing for a strategic career change. Far too many of us tend to hold tight to avoid confrontations with our own long-run situation and end up disillusioned and baffled when our careers have ended.

Determine the Total Price

The maturity of unions and their members in facing the devastating effect of wages that priced their employers out of world markets stands as a shining testimonial to the necessity of confrontational management. Wage give-backs are not popular, and dissidents within the ranks are sure to use the issue to undermine and attempt to unseat the union leadership. It takes a man like Douglas Fraser to see the need for realistic negotiations when jobs are being exported because American labor isn't competitive. Collective bargaining, which consists of a joint agreement between unions and employers to raise wages and pass the resulting cost increases on to consumers, doesn't work when the consumers have the option of buying cheaper foreign products.

Personal careers likewise call for a price to be paid. You might try getting on in your career while living a life of ignoble ease, never missing a golf game, pretending that everything will come out OK. But life will probably disabuse you of the value of such an approach when you end up working for those who put in the time, the energy, and the commitment to perform and contribute at a higher level. The person who doesn't want to pay the price may find a comfortable shelf to rest upon but will be missing an important fact about confrontation if he or she supposes that good things come to those who sit around waiting for them.

You can't move ahead by being a chronic critic and debunker of everything that's new. You can scoff at the rising importance of the computer, or you can take a course and learn what these machines are all about. This is a price you pay.

You might pretend—or hope—that changes in human relations at work, such as affirmative action and age discrimination laws, will be abolished and then do your best to assure that such abolition happens. But if in the process you've been unwilling to pay the toughest price of all by adapting to the changes while working for their reversal, then you have failed to confront reality.

Chris Argyris once said that people should learn to compete

without displaying hostility, and this is still pretty good advice. The whole idea of confrontation is not to become a chronic battler, wearing hostility on your shoulder like an epaulet, but to face up to the realities of modern managerial life.

Cooperation Is Superior to Confrontation

Although I have cited the advantages of using confrontation when the situation calls for it, the best advice still remains: Talk your way out of situations, if possible, before you start your guns blazing.

Cooperation and collaboration are still the most civilized ways of getting where you want to go, and the people who choose to fight first and talk later usually end up broken or dead. By finding common areas of agreement and seeking unity of effort, you can avoid the damage which often accompanies head-on battles.

Fighting when the same result could have been achieved by giving a little in negotiation is wasteful and produces a lose–lose outcome. Victory and defeat are terms that have strong emotional overtones. If you lose today and seek revenge and victory tomorrow, you're only preparing the way for a still larger counterresponse in the future. Negotiation produces a win–win outcome.

Confrontation is most useful in dealing with troubles, problems, situations, and challenges. It's usually counterproductive in dealing with people. Deal with people one-on-one, eyeball-to-eyeball, then take a break, caucus, and see if something of a collaborative nature can't be worked out.

Don't be afraid to allow other people to vent their anger without becoming angry yourself. Even though anger begets anger, the fact that somebody has blasted you in anger doesn't have to trigger an angry response. Your anger will only produce a similar reaction in others which will rip the possibility of settlement to shreds.

Never engage in a confrontation with someone when you are angry. Take time to cool off and act rationally. Confrontation requires cool thought to resolve a situation, not emotional binges.

Part II
Successful
Goal Setting

———————

Over the years I've regularly asked my key people—and I've had them ask their key people, and so on down the line—a few basic questions: "What are your objectives for the next ninety days? What are your plans, your priorities, your hopes? And how do you intend to go about achieving them?"

—Lee Iacocca

5
Goals: The Building Blocks for Integration and Self-Control

Don't waste time talking about what you have already done. Use the
time executing or planning something new.

—Eugene Grace

I n the world of bureaucracy there are order givers and order takers. While this is very efficient because it divides the labor cleanly,
thus allowing people to acquire skills and specialization, it is also
highly depersonalized. Workers, customers, and bosses all become
instrumental to the purposes of the organization. The more efficient
the bureaucracy becomes, the more the people involved become
numbers. Social Security, employee identification, credit cards, li-
censes, area codes, zip codes—all are designed to reduce the complexity of a human being to a manageable dimension expressed as
a number. In numerous ways the structure of an organization creates a loss of the individual's identity, and this is turn creates a par-
adox. We organize for efficiency and in the process so depersonalize
individuals and their humanity that they become angry, apathetic,
or alienated. Such people thus become both the product of the bureaucracy and the cause of its lost effectiveness and eventual demise.

The Activity Trap

Some of the largest and most affluent corporations are caught in an
insidious trap. It is called the Activity Trap, and it afflicts small and
large corporations alike. It even extends beyond the business world
to government, schools, hospitals, churches, even families. Unless
victims are aware of it, the Activity Trap will ensnare the wisest,
most experienced old hands.

The Activity Trap is the abysmal situation people find themselves in when they start out toward an important and clear objective but, in an amazingly short time, become so enmeshed in the activity of getting there that they forget where they are going.

Every business organization starts out to achieve some objective, usually to increase profits. Resources are assembled from stockholders, loans, or savings, and poured into the enterprise. Everyone gets busy, engaging in activity designed to carry the organization toward its objectives. Once-clear goals may evolve into something else, while the activity remains the same—and becomes an end in itself. In other words, the activity persists, but toward a *false* goal.

A bus driver in England was reported to have driven past numerous passengers waiting at various bus stops, even though his bus was not full. When asked for an explanation, the company replied, "If we were to stop for all passengers we wouldn't be able to maintain our schedule."

Quality control directors often act as if enterprise were created so they could shut it down and hold up everything that was produced yesterday.

The accountant acts as if the business were created so that he could keep books on it. No longer does he keep books so that the boss can better run the business.

The sales manager acts as if there were no problems that couldn't be solved by more volume. Sales go up, but profits fall.

Production workers get tonnage out the back gate by shipping junk.

Personnel managers behave as if the entire purpose of hiring employees was to keep the personnel department employed.

Churches become enmeshed with covered-dish suppers and basketball leagues—activities generating little other than indigestion and flat feet.

Families get so entangled in the mechanical processes of living that they forget the importance of loving and caring.

Service clubs spend more and more time exhorting members to "support this activity" with no hint of a worthwhile payoff.

Meanwhile all this activity eats up resources, money, space, budgets, savings, and human energy like a mammoth tapeworm.

This process of "goals displacement," as Robert Merton once called it, means that people can't be integrated into the entire organization; their personal goals can't be related to organization goals, and the work of smaller units aren't integrated with the larger goals of the organization.

While it's apparent that the Activity Trap cuts profits, loses ball games, and fails to achieve missions, it has an equally dangerous side effect on people; they *shrink* personally and professionally.

The People Shrinker

Take any boss and one of his or her subordinates. Ask the employee to write down what specific results this boss wants him to produce in the next quarter. Now ask the boss, "What results would you like to see that person produce next quarter?" Although the average manager and subordinate may be reasonably close on *activities* to be conducted, they won't agree on *results sought*. Answers will differ, and such differences will prevent the subordinate from living up to his or her potential. Research shows that on regular, ongoing responsibilities the average boss and subordinate, caught in the Activity Trap, will fail to agree on expected outputs at a level of 25 percent. As a result, they will also disagree on what the subordinate's major problems are, at a level of 50 percent.

The worst gap of all is failure of boss and subordinate to agree on how the subordinate's job should be improved. This means that nothing really changes in the way things are done. The environment changes, customers' tastes change, the values of employees change. But the methods remain static and the organization crippled by the outdated acts of its own employees.

The human consequence is that the employees *shrink*. The organization drains its people of their zap and finds itself employing pygmies. They look like normal-size people, wear shoes, drive cars, and pay taxes, but they are performance pygmies. They nod their heads when the boss chastises them, but know they have been cheated. They are stabbed daily in duels they didn't know were under way. Trees fall upon them, and then somebody yells "Timber!" Their defensive recourse? Keep active.

They redouble their energy even though they have lost sight of their goal. They may be chastised, or even fired, for doing something wrong when they didn't know what right was to begin with. They run a race without knowing how long the track is.

The effect is cumulative. Because the employees don't know the ordinary objectives of their jobs they are hit for failures resulting from ignorance of what constitutes success. This produces a reluctance to discover problems, for the problems they discover might be attributed to their own shortcomings. Suggesting something new in such an environment is also risky. Better to stick with the old activity. Looking busy becomes safer than being productive.

Antidotes to Bureaucracy

The behavioral sciences have long been attracted to the problem of managing humans at work. The discontent of the bureaucratic worker enmeshed in the Activity Trap has been the subject of many studies and solutions. Three major categories of antidote have emerged, along with many minor ones.

For some, decentralization and delegation has proven to be a helpful antidote. Giant organizations are broken down into smaller divisions, with a general manager in charge. This manager has wide authority to make decisions at the local business or market level. This means that the decision maker can be more visible to the people affected by those decisions.

Human relations training, with numerous variations, has a forty-year history of attempting to change managerial behavior to a style more pleasing to those being managed.

My own proposal is on a more immediate one-on-one basis between every boss and every subordinate. It has been called Management by Objectives (MBO). Other names exist for the same idea. At General Electric it is Working Planning and Review. Consultant Ed Schleh, a pioneer in its application at 3M, calls it Managing for Results. At Eastman Kodak it is Results Managing.

The label isn't important. The basic idea is that every boss and subordinate will negotiate objectives at the beginning of each period, sometimes quarterly, sometimes annually. Such negotiation is a formal planned discussion of goals, results sought, priorities, and plans. It is, to my mind, the most intensive system devised for producing management by integration and self-control. The goals discussions integrate the work and plans of the subordinate with those of the organization. By agreeing in advance and making a commitment to goals, the subordinate can operate freely under self-control.

First the two parties meet face-to-face to discuss the responsibilities of the subordinate's job, its goals and expected results and indicators, until they agree on what the future will hold. One of the parties then confirms the agreement with a memo. Now when the curtain goes up both actors have the same script. This improves the quality of the acting considerably. The emphasis is on outputs, not activities. Every person knows what is expected of him or her and can tell immediately how well he or she is doing. They know they are responsible for results and have committed themselves to trying to achieve the objectives.

At the end of the period, the manager and subordinate sit down once more and talk again. "Here is what you said you were going to produce. How well did you do, and what are you going to do next quarter?"

The key man in this type of productive organization is the top man. He determines that the organization will be managed by objectives, not activity. He determines the corporate objectives and strategic goals. The subordinate managers define their operational objectives to fit those top-level goals and strategies. The top man should not be involved in day-to-day operations but should manage them by the objectives he has set.

Nonbusiness organizations need explicit objectives too. Families with defined objectives can get off the backs of their offspring, permitting wider latitudes in activity and behavior if the end result is good.

MBO is management orthodoxy these days. The majority of the Fortune 500 companies manage their major divisions by objectives, even though many of these same firms don't always apply MBO all the way down into the ranks of supervision. More than half of the 300-bed and larger hospitals in the United States manage by objectives, and MBO has been introduced with fairly consistent results in government and other nonprofit organizations.

Eight Reasons for Goal Setting

Here are eight clear reasons why you should manage your affairs, including your career, by objectives:

1. The human being is a purposive being. People live to attain goals. They set them and create them both on their own and on suggestion from others. T.A. Ryan suggests that all behavior is purposive, and thus MBO is easily related to instinctual as well as learned and acquired behavior.

2. Organizations have a tendency to disperse this purposiveness. By the mechanics of the division of labor which produces efficiency through organization, people can get caught in an activity trap. The work takes control and the goals get lost unless managers systematically keep pulling people back to goals and objectives by asking again and again: "What are we in business for? What are the purposes of this organization? What goods or services are we trying to produce? Who is our client? Why is this work or this expenditure necessary? What will the outcome be if we succeed (or fail)?"

3. Managers and bosses in organizations lose sight of subordinate goals. Left to their own devices, the average manager and subordinate, busy at activity, will have quite different ideas about what the subordinate's responsibilities are for the coming year. This means that compensation is paid for activity that has no yield the boss wants or the organization can use. The subordinate works hard rather than productively. Mutually agreed-upon goals are needed.

4. People caught in an activity trap shrink rather than grow as human beings. When people get enmeshed in activity instead of focusing upon objectives, their effectiveness (the attainment of goals) diminishes exactly to the extent that they are unclear about where they are going. If you aim for nothing, that is what you will hit.

Hard work that produces failures yields apathy, inertia, and lost self-esteem. The growth of self-esteem (the feeling of liking oneself) comes from setting good, exciting, or even noble objectives and then attaining all or most of them. People become instrumental, demeaned, and diminished as humans when their work proves later to have been largely (or even partially) without meaning . . . without a goal.

5. Failure can consist of failing to achieve goals, or it can consist of never knowing what the goals were. In either event the tragedy is both economic (the company or organization loses out in the marketplace or in the competition for operating funds) and humanistic (people who work in a failing organization are diminished and often destroyed). The great tragedy of a bankruptcy like that of W.T. Grant is not limited to stockholders but is shared by the "stakeholders"—the firm's customers, suppliers, and most especially the employees. Unclear objectives produce more failures than incompetence, malfeasance, misfeasance, or bad luck combined.

6. Performance improves when people know what their goals are. The best motivator is pure, raw information. ("Here is what is expected of you in your work in specific terms of outputs for a specific period of time.") When people learn this valuable information they change their behavior, attain the skills needed to attain the goals to which they are committed, and adapt themselves to change without consciously thinking about it. In retrospect they discern that they have grown.

7. Ethical behavior is more likely to be surrounded by goal attainment than by preachers and moralistic lecturers. The business that has lost sight of its goals is likely to go broke. The nonprofit organization that has failed to enlist others clearly in the pursuit of its goals is likely to become extinct. A failing organization is more likely to cut corners or to cheat its suppliers, customers, and employees than is an organization that is doing well. Generally speaking, the more an organization is worth, the more worthy it becomes.

8. Most management subsystems succeed or fail according to the clarity of overall goals of the organization. Without clear goals in the hands of all employees and managers the organization cannot operate a decent merit system of rewards in wages and benefits, validate its psychological tests, dispense its budget resources sensi-

bly and effectively, or plan its future. Goal setting is sufficiently vital that it becomes a necessary if not sufficient condition for management to occur at all. MBO isn't an addition to a manager's job but a way of doing that job.

With such an eminently logical rationale in hand, the question of how to set goals remains. "I'm persuaded by the logic and rationality of it all, but I see many detailed skill problems in defining goals in my situation," the typical manager says. "Are there some guidelines for goal setting?"

6
Where Do Specific Objectives Come From?

It is better to limp on the right way than to run on the wrong.
—John Calvin

Integration means that the goals chosen through negotiation meet the needs of both the subordinate and the organization. It is in these agreements that integration and self-control are forged.

It is the job of the boss to assure that the objectives agreed upon—committed to—fulfill the requirements of the organization. In some organizations the objectives are for profit; in others, for service. Some goals will be stated in terms of tangible outputs called hardware. In other jobs, the subordinate produces advice, service, information, or new knowledge called software. Thus Xerox may set goals for profit, sales, market share, productivity. It will also set goals for such areas as employee development, new systems, product development, or relationships with the public. The Veterans' Administration has goals of restoring health and providing for other needs of those who served their country. Police departments have goals of maintaining the public safety.

It is during the face-to-face discussion between boss and subordinate that the goals will be created and forged. Until the two have agreed, the goals don't exist, are fuzzy, or even irrelevant.

Good goals are the key to success in managing by objectives, but where do you find them? Many courses in MBO teach how best to describe objectives once they have been decided upon. This is an essential skill in goal setting, but an ability to find the right goals to begin with is even more important. Where does an organization—or an individual manager—find the best goals?

If the wrong goals are set, the perfect execution of an MBO program will only produce a well-executed fiasco rather than a stunning victory. The starting place for finding the right objectives is probably within the organization itself for most managers. But for the organization as a whole, the search must cover both internal and external factors and influences in order to identify opportunities.

Finding good goals usually starts with the right attitude at the top of the organization. A management which lacks a believing attitude probably won't set very noble or ambitious goals, and the results will show the effects of such timidity. As Alice said in her dialogue with the Red Queen, "One can't believe impossible things." Many managers start out believing that anything new is, by definition, impossible.

The first step in goal-finding is to imagine the impossible, and then to abandon it only when hard study shows that it really is impossible. David Sarnoff built RCA by motivating his research scientists to imagine the impossible: the electron microscope, color television, and dozens of other devices which we now take for granted.

It's not easy to find new goals if you are insecure. Insecure people attract and keep other insecure people around them and meet all of their needs by losing. I know one firm in which the real, though unwritten, company motto is "I think I can't." This is bound to be a self-fulfilling prophecy.

Managers who have a high level of what David McClelland calls achievement motivation believe that they will succeed, though upsets will occur, and that winners are those who are most often sure that they can win.

Ten Places to Look for Goals

1. Problems

The most likely place to find a good goal is right within your own situation. Problems make excellent goals, and every organization has plenty of problems. If quality has slipped or if accidents are rising, turn these problems into objectives.

The high rate of business failures, continuing high levels of unemployment, and the persistent rise of foreign competition are all part of the problem-finding basket into which you can reach to seek out some worthy goals for the organization and for its people. Japanese businessmen live in a world where they have few natural resources and where energy costs eat up most of their export balances, but they attack the problems with a will and get everyone committed to their game plan. Our own firms which continue to do well in the face of foreign competition are those that turn such problems into goals.

It's been said that every problem is an opportunity turned inside out.

2. Product Line

Assess your product line systematically to find objectives. Try classifying your products by age on a product life cycle curve. There are four categories on such a curve: (a) start-up products, (b) growth products, (c) mature products, and (d) declining products. The very act of placing each product from your complete line into one of these categories will suggest some meaningful goals in building a balanced mix.

You can then set objectives to introduce new products, push growth products, cash in on mature products, and divest those products which are in the later stages of decline.

Use hard numbers to make your classifications. Facts are the building blocks of good goals.

3. Strengths and Weaknesses

Gather your senior people together and construct an internal assessment of these two questions: What are the major strengths we should be building on? What weaknesses do we have that we should be shoring up with protective goals?

The answers to these questions will provide more than enough objectives for your key people. Break the tasks down and assign the parts to responsible persons. People who help in answering these questions will be more impelled to work on the goals which flow from them.

4. Portfolio Analysis

Do a portfolio analysis of your product line, markets, business opportunities, divisions, and personnel. The idea, adapted from the Boston Consulting Group's method for analyzing a stock portfolio, is to rate products (or whatever) on two scales, placing each into one of four categories.

For example, you might rate products on the basis of market growth and market share in the following manner: A product that is low both on market growth and on market share is classified as a "dog" and should be divested. A product that is high both on market growth and market share is a "star" which should be polished. A product with a high market share but that is in a no-growth or low-growth market is a "cash cow" to be milked. And a product in a high-growth market with which you have a low market share is a "problem child"; your goals here is to make the problem child into a star or, failing that, to divest it.

In a portfolio analysis of your human resources you might rate people on the basis of present performance and potential for advancement.

5. Cost Reduction

Cost reduction programs are always a ripe field for finding goals, and indeed every MBO program these days should include some cost reduction goals. Make it an objective to get a higher yield from the same resources, and assign targets to responsible people.

When costs get out of line, apply the Rule of 20/80. That is, 80 percent of any excessive costs can usually be found to be caused by 20 percent of the organizational units. Focus on those high-cost units rather than applying cost reduction programs across the board.

For instance, 80 percent of overtime costs are usually generated by two out of ten departments and 80 percent of accidents are generally found to occur on only 20 percent of the jobs. Knowing which departments are big spenders for overtime and which occupations are most accident-prone, you can focus your cost reduction efforts and safety programs on these key departments and occupations.

Focus your goals on the vital few rather than the trivial many.

6. Cut Your Losses

Every firm and every department should have a program stated in its objectives for working its way out of its least productive activities. This doesn't suggest that you run about with a meat-ax, but rather that you have a goal of getting out of your least productive businesses or activities.

We all know how hard it is to abandon something which has been around for a long time. It's best done gradually, using a time-phased plan. Perhaps the business was founded on a product which has lost its appeal but to which many people in the organization are emotionally attached. Use your portfolio analysis and life cycle analysis to pick out the losers to be dropped.

Make somebody responsible for producing an orderly plan to get out of losing ventures. Put a freeze on expenditures and capital budgets for losing businesses so as not to throw away good money after bad. Don't hire people for nonessential positions when the last person to hold the job leaves or retires. Learn to say no.

7. Opportunities

In picking opportunity targets, always examine a lot of options. The element of risk in goal setting comes when you are choosing which opportunities to exploit. Solid staff work really pays off here.

More new products fail than succeed, usually due to inadequate study. Proctor & Gamble has a superior track record in introducing new products precisely because it does such a superior job in studying products and markets first. They look for a market that is large enough to be worth entering, then choose to enter only when they have a product with some technical advantage visible to buyers and after they have devised a plan that will assure them a substantial share of the market.

Whether you're starting a new business, introducing a new product or service, buying a house, or picking a spouse, check out many options before making your decision. In business matters, assign studies of various options to professionals. The fact that a study may result in a negative conclusion doesn't mean that the study wasn't worthwhile. The objective of investigating to produce a stop-or-go decision is extremely valuable for selecting opportunities to exploit.

8. Human Resources Development

Human resources development should always be included in your objectives. If such matters don't flow up naturally from the bottom along with reports of financial and marketing objectives, send the report back to have the human resources development objectives added. All managers should be required to state development objectives for themselves as well as for their key subordinates.

Construct a human resources portfolio identifying your stars, workhorses, problem children, and deadwood. Then make certain that objectives for each person are stated as part of the business plan. Don't sit still for generalizations as developmental goals. Build your stars for the future. Improve the performance of your workhorses on present jobs. Straighten out your problem children. Move your deadwood out of their present positions.

9. Motivation

Require that motivational goals be included in every MBO plan. Ask managers to explain how they intend to build teamwork, how they will provide information to people on what is expected of them, how incentives will be developed and used, and how opportunities will be exploited to stimulate the best performance from every subordinate. If managers don't present such motivational goals in their MBO statements, talk to them and suggest that they do more thinking along these lines.

Uncover the obstacles which are stopping the workhorses from growing on their present jobs and which are holding back the stars from living up to their full potential. In earlier days, Henry Ford II would ask his division managers if they had any people like Lee Iacocca out there and what they were doing to develop them. That's the sort of question each manager should be expected to answer. ("Who are your best people and what are your present plans for their growth and development in terms of promotions, special challenging assignments, courses and seminars, and so on?")

10. Commitment

Insist that every manager use objectives as the key element in his or her managerial system. Don't let some wheeler-dealer operate without specific commitments. Make it clear that people work in a goals-driven organization by making it mandatory that the manager's job include: (1) stating overall organizational strategies and operating goals in writing, and (2) obtaining similar sets of goals from each subordinate manager.

As one president told his division manager: "I won't tell you what your goals should be, but one alternative which isn't open to any of us is that of operating without a clear statement about what we intend to accomplish during the coming year." The days of the intuitive hotshot are numbered. You need to make it clear that goals are mandatory, not voluntary. The specifics of the goals can be left to lower levels, but goals are a must.

Finding good goals is more important than writing them down well. People who ask the right questions and who use facts to define options and make decisions will do better than people who only respond to crises from the past. Goals should make things happen, not merely forecast what will happen regardless of whether something is written down in advance or not. Challenge your managers to be deciders, not drifters.

Good job objectives don't arise from a form of power brokering; they spring from a lively imagination. The modern organization has a serious need for imagination, intelligence, and discretionary judgment, and you can't order that into existence. Nor can you get it by exchanging memos. Imagination doesn't respond to commands or money, at least not consistently. If it is to exist at all it must be voluntarily produced. Try to generate it bureaucratically and it may appear, but usually it won't (as thousands of disheartened middle managers, tangled in organizational red tape, prove daily.)

People can be exhorted to *think,* and once in a while the exhortation works. But the best fruits of the human mind—the creativity and innovation needed to cope with inflation, war, poverty, energy crises, and world food shortages—will come only when the owners of the brains want to produce new ideas.

An MBO program which aims at producing more managerial control is nothing more than a substitute for a labor gang foreman in a lumberjack operation. It simply won't do for managing educated people with degrees in engineering, accounting, finance, or science whose contribution lies in their intelligence and imagination. You can't beat the hell out of middle-class professionals and then expect creative ideas to flow like physical labor from a gang of hired hands.

If it's wit, wisdom, cleverness, ingenuity, imagination, and innovation you hope to tease out of your team of professional managers in the form of new goals, exciting objectives, and noble aims, you must do it on a personal, one-on-one basis.

Unless MBO produces such personal contacts between superior and subordinate managers, the whole affair becomes another exercise in bureaucratic rubbish.

To Whom Do You Look for Goals?

To find organizational goals, look to the top person first. When Orville Beal became president of Prudential, it was number two in the insurance industry, behind the giant Metropolitan. Beal made it clear that his ambition was to become number one. This dominant goal became the building block for all other objectives of the firm. Before he retired, Beal was able to realize his goal. It was this goal, in fact, that produced the real zeal, effort, and ingenuity that got Prudential to the number one spot.

Charlie Revson, as he was dying, picked Michael Bergerac out of ITT's European subsidiary as his successor because Bergerac knew how to make money by the bundle by keeping the company attuned to the market and its wants. Bergerac outdid his predecessor and made Revlon one of the most profitable firms of the seventies. While holding onto Revlon's fragrance business, Bergerac engineered a $400 million merger with Technicon, a leader in medical diagnostics, and in the process moved Revlon into a new and extremely profitable line of business. He doubled sales and tripled profits. At the same time, he replaced Revson's temper-tantrum style of management with a more goals-centered, decentralized style.

At McDonald's it was the compelling leadership of Ray Kroc that produced a 35 percent compound annual earning increase during the last half of the seventies.

From Moses to Pierre du Pont, history proves the crucial role of the top person in creating goals for the organization.

Where does this top person find such magic goals? Usually in the market place, whence goals ultimately come.

While it's easier to choose lofty or noble goals if your top person is a dynamic leader, it seems to be a fair substitute to have two people whose joint abilities produce imaginative and impelling goals. Some firms have been started by partners whose capabilities, though different, comprised an unbeatable combination.

Gordon Moore and Robert Noyce left Fairchild to provide a heavy punch at Intel, the Santa Clara, California, maker of computer chips and microprocessors. When Noyce, a top technical inventor, moved into a less compelling role, his place was taken by Andrew Grove, also from Fairchild.

Aetna moved into a unique and strong position in the general financial field during the seventies with a rather special kind of "office of the president" arrangement, with three persons in charge rather than one, which was in place during much of the transition period.

General Electric likewise went through such a phase during the change in leadership following Fred Borch into the Reginald Jones era. Three executives shared the top office, rather than one.

Many a small firm has prospered because one partner handled sales and finance while the other managed engineering and manufacturing. To make this system work it is important that the two or three top people communicate on an open and complete level, and that doesn't happen automatically. It calls for some special personal chemistry.

Though goal-finding centers at the top, it can be more widely shared. Sometimes an organization's objectives are a summation of individual objectives. Richard Cyert and J.G. March, in their book *The Behavioral Theory of the Firm,* avow that there are no such things as a firm's goals, only a "negotiated consensus of influential participants."

In such a scheme, the goals and strategies of the firm are a product of the needs and desires of all the interested stakeholders. There are stockholders who want earnings and growth, employees who want high wages, customers who want quality products at low prices, and a public that wants a good environment and law-abiding companies.

Such a system involves a lot of participation. Sales goals are usually composed of forecasts from the sales force. Production goals are the combined estimates and plans of production people. The general approach is bottom-up rather than top-down, with plenty of time and space for discussion and debate before goals are set. The resulting goals are not perfect; they represent only compromise and reconciliation.

The payoff from such a system isn't found in the quality of goals but in the wide acceptance of the targets throughout the organization. This acceptance flows from the consensus approach to goal setting, producing more enthusiastic and intelligent execution. Thus it ends up being the best of all forms.

The Heart of Goal Setting

The much-talked-about office of the future will soon be here. You will talk into a machine which will produce on mag-cards for correction a complete transcript of what you have on your mind. Magic cables will carry information to other people, make multiple copies, and record everything on a cathode memory tube. All this and much much more will comprise the information revolution, we are told.

If we don't watch our steps as we race into the future, however, we may lose sight of what makes the management process work, and especially that part of the process which has to do with goal setting—the face-to-face discussion between boss and subordinate.

Regardless of whether written communications are automated or old-fashioned, the MBO process centers on two live people talking to one another. The product of the confab will be confirmed in writing (typed, handwritten, word-processed, or sent by telenet). But without the face-to-face discussion, the whole soul and substance of MBO are lost.

Goal setting in an MBO system is a process of people talking to people and bargaining with people. Sometimes this bargaining is based on the authority of the boss to make final decisions. Sometimes it involves patching up disagreements between boss and subordinate over what is realistic and attainable in the job environment. And sometimes it's aimed at changing the behavior of the subordinate. The face-to-face process cannot be eliminated or reduced in any of these three kinds of discussion—bargaining, conflict resolution, or behavior change.

When people talk face-to-face they can communicate. Communication, it is said, is behavior that produces an exchange of meaning. Bosses can hear and observe how people feel during a face-to-face discussion—something that can't be done interfacing with a memo or some electronic device.

The recent rash of firings of top executives at CBS, RCA, and Coca-Cola occurred, according to my information, only after the key people involved had stopped communicating fully face-to-face. This can happen at any level—president and vice president, general manager and department head, superintendent and foreman.

When two people stop talking, their relationship is certain to produce failure. If the relationship between a boss and subordinate is so formal that they have to rely upon written memos alone, the MBO process is dead.

Without face-to-face contact built irrevocably and faithfully into your MBO system, it doesn't matter how neatly your MBO plan is constructed. The idea of MBO as a system of management is not to create a reporting plan or to construct a logical management information system. MBO builds human relationships.

7
Organization-wide Integration through MBO

The greatest organization is that which enables the greatest percentage of those in the business to receive in earnings that which they actually make, that is, to have a system that measures each person's results.
—Eugene Grace

Y ou can produce integration in two ways: accidentally or on purpose. Management by integration and self-control might be left to each supervisor and each manager as a discretionary matter. This would call for a great deal of self-training by supervisors, supplemented by constant reminders and exhortation. Every time a new person joined the management team he or she would have to be trained and exhorted anew. The alternative is the creation of a formal system which has as its objective the integration of the goals of the organization and those of the subordinates. Management by objectives, with its variations, purports to be such a system and is widely employed to achieve the goal of integration.

Filley and House summarized research on the impact that goal setting has upon integration of organizational and personal goals. They found four propositions to be evident:

1. The pursuit of values in the form of customer or client satisfaction is a needed function of the organization if it is to survive and be profitable.

2. If organizations operate with goals that are consistently offensive to society or conflict with social mores, undesirable consequences will result.

3. Clear organization goals to which individuals are expected to contribute directly will improve individual contributions and cooperative effort.

4. When contribution to organization objectives is consistent
with personal goals, member motivation to work and member satisfaction with the organization will be high.

Make Organization-wide Goal Setting a Reality

A sometime effort depending upon the voluntary behavior of individual managers won't by itself be enough to make integration and
self-control the prevailing style of management and maximize its
benefits to the individual and the organization. The organization
itself must adopt the policy of setting its own goals. Simply expect-
ing managers to reinvent the concept of goals-driven management
will cause the concept and philosophy to languish. The activity trap
will take over. A sequence of events is required to make organization-wide goal setting a reality.

1. *Start at the top.* The beginning point is at the top of the
organization. Usually this entails a kind of familiarization training
for the officers or senior managers of the organization. This will be
corporate-level officers if the system is to be corporation-wide. The
reason for this is clear. It is at the top that the strategic goals and
missions of firms are determined, and strategies are important as
guides to the goals of lower ranks.

2. *Adopt a policy.* Policy is a guide to action, and if goal setting
is to be the common unifying management system for the entire
organization, this must be stated as a policy and communicated to
the entire management team.

3. *Strategic goals and missions must cascade downward.* Lee
Iacocca said it was his practice to sit down with the managers who
reported directly to him and with their own direct subordinates.

4. *Training is needed.* Formal, planned training programs in the
methods of goal setting, including some understanding of the philosophy and concepts involved, are required if success is to follow.
In cases where selected top officers actively participate in such training, acceptance by subordinates is higher. Officers indicate that they
not only permit but endorse goal setting by training subordinates
to set goals. This adds impetus to lower-level goal setting.

In May and Company, the giant retailer, chief executive officer Dave Babcock took an active part in the conduct of training for lower levels. The impact upon supervisory and staff people from this personal involvement of the chief executive officer produced a strong and supportive engagement of those so trained. The results in growth and profit in the firm were attributed in large part by Babcock to his personal endorsement and support of goals-driven management.

5. *Continual follow-up*. Programs for management by integration and self-control are not self-executing. When problems arise, they must be resolved. For many firms this has been the responsibility of a corporate or organizational MBO administrator who deals with system problems, trains people in new methods and techniques, and researches the effects to uncover potential problems. At Tenneco, Inc., the Houston conglomerate, administrator William Streidl commonly invites outside researchers into the firm to evaluate the effectiveness of the corporate MBO program.

6. *Program administration must be competent*. The mechanics of handling performance reviews, of conducting group goal-setting sessions, of the design and execution of training, and organization development training must be competently directed. The role of MBO administrator then is that of internal consultant, which demands special expertise in the system, its problems, and the means of alleviating difficulties as they arise. Often a manager with line experience and skills as a facilitator is a competent MBO administrator.

Prevention of apathy once the program is under way remains a chronic concern. Many MBO programs have been launched with considerable fanfare and sold through exhortation, only to fade away as daily business pressures impinge upon the requirements of MBO management. Individual supervisors may feel threatened and show faint enthusiasm. People in the lower ranks who lack confidence in their own abilities may challenge the whole process and withhold their commitment to goal setting. How does a company cope with such erosion of original interest and enthusiasm?

Focus on the Important

Starting goal setting at the top of an organization has a very special kind of logic. A letter from the president to the entire managerial team helps focus everyone's attention on those problems, weaknesses, strengths, and opportunities that need the cooperation and involvement of the entire team.

For example, the director of a state department of public health focused everyone's attention upon infant mortality. Regional chiefs and local supervisors all knew that they should include among their other goals some new ideas, strong programs, and imaginative plans for reducing infant mortality and, further, that such goals should be near the top. A lot of kids are alive today because the director focused upon that goal.

Another example can be found in the auto company where the president communicated his priorities for the corporation through a twenty-minute film made expressly for that purpose.

In a smaller organization the president can communicate what's important directly through personal talks with his or her managers, covering both a personal philosophy of management and the purposes of the organization.

The best time to do this is in midyear, just before the budget-setting process gets under way. People who know about new and heightened priorities can devise plans and objectives that are in tune with those priorities. They can then adapt their budget requests to move resources to the high-priority items.

Budget committee members who allocate funds should be clear in their priorities and approve those programs that seem to promise the greatest contribution to goals.

Every manager's goals are unique and should be tailored to the needs of the organization. Managers should avoid copycatting; that is, they shouldn't just hold onto last year's goals for another year, nor should they use the goals of their counterparts in another organization. For one thing, different organizations have different economic drives; both need goals that are tailored to their needs.

The growth business is very much concerned with increasing its market share and with seeking out the very best people almost regardless of pay, without worrying much about investment levels, fixing costs too tightly, or making perfect products the first time around. It goes for market position and uses its working capital (cash receivables and inventory) to grab market share.

The mature business, on the other hand, needs iron control over working capital, and inventory, along with tight cash-management systems and firm credit-management plans. Profits and profitability are of greater concern than market position for these firms that seek to cut fixed costs, keep investments in new equipment as low as possible, and stress cost reduction programs.

If your business is one which is heavily capitalized, it would be a good idea to make keeping the plant running at full capacity an overall goal of every manager. Don't throw good money after bad by trying to shore up your weak spots, but rather build on your strengths.

Every business goes through a number of stages, from start-up to growth, maturity, and decline. You should know where your business and its various segments stand in this cycle and you should have your managers set objectives consistent with the kind of business you are in, not for the fellow across the street or the guy who made the great speech at the trade association convention last year. Good goals are tailored to your own business and should call for experience and judgment about what is important and what isn't.

Reward Risk Takers

The best strategic planning system requires that you have innovative risk-taking managers in lower ranks who will keep proposing new ideas to those above them. While it's true that the objectives of lower-level managers are primarily routine, it is important to ask every manager to accept some problem-solving and innovative objectives.

Large organizations need a steady supply of entrepreneurial people at lower levels who are pressing for change, improvement, and innovation, because many of these organizations are top-heavy in staff experts who specialize in squelching new ideas. What you need are risk takers in management. When you find them, don't chill their creativity and innovative ideas.

Here is how you can nurture and develop risk-taking proposals from below:

1. Learn to recognize the "plungers" (people who would take unwarranted risks without full study), the "stand-patters" (who never take a chance on anything), and "reasonable adventurers" (who propose reasonable and prudent risks based upon full study and a dash of daring).

2. If you want innovation, ask for it. The assumption that innovation is bursting to spring into action and produce great things for the organization won't lead to productive change unless people are told explicitly that innovative thinking is expected of them.

3. Reward innovation. Not only should the pay and merit system encourage innovative behavior but the intangible rewards system should also favor people who innovate. If you're not getting more good ideas from the lower ranks than you can handle, you may have a stifling climate that needs modification.

4. Get commitments from people to convert natural tendencies to seek variety and innovation into concrete suggestions, ideas, and actual changes. The use of face-to-face discussion to ask people about opportunities that might be exploited is another step toward creation of a general climate in which innovation can flourish.

5. Train people in work simplification, methods improvement, value engineering, and creative thinking, as a way of telling them that change is desired and that the status quo isn't good enough.

6. The personal support of the manager is crucial. Innovation becomes an organizational way of life when the boss sits down regularly with subordinates to stress the importance of innovation and ask for commitments to innovative objectives, and then follows up by endorsing, supporting, and rewarding innovation.

7. Don't let too many chronic nay-sayers get into top spots. Top management must share the risks with the innovative people from below. When you see a decisive, innovative lower-level manager, encourage his or her innovation.

Set Tough, Clear Goals

A young farmer bought a run-down farm and overhauled it completely, mainly by hard work. One day the county agent dropped by and commended him: "Young man, I gotta say, you and the Lord have done wonders with this old farm." The farmer thought for a moment, then replied: "Thanks for the nice words, but did you see this place when the Lord was workin' it by himself?" The point, of course, is that most success is self-created. Similarly, most successful management development is self-development.

It would be nonsense to suggest that such a thing as luck doesn't exist, but luck isn't the dominant influence over success and failure for most people in most jobs.

Psychologist David McClelland's studies indicate clearly that people of moderate aspirations are apt to achieve moderate results, while people with high levels of achievement motivation accomplish much more. They develop greater confidence in their own abilities and, when faced with a new and untried goal, they are better able than most people to achieve it. Achievers are goal setters who speak the language of success, not failure. Achievers relate better to their environment than do others around them.

If you aim for nothing, that is just about what you'll get. If you aim for a little, you get a little. If you aim for a lot, work hard, and live up to your potential, you achieve a lot.

Success, then, is related to setting job objectives. Without objectives there is no success.

Set Tangible, Measurable Goals

Managerial objectives are easier to agree upon when the goals are tangible and measurable. You can prevent a lot of problems with MBO if you can use dollars, pounds, units, a ratio of some kind, a scale of measurement, or some other tangible measurement of output. The major problem you will prevent is that which arises when the time comes to tell people whether or not they have met their goals. Obviously a measurable objective is easier to track than an unmeasurable one.

That's why IBM sets quotas for its salespeople consisting of specific targets which are either met or not met. If the quota is not met, a plausible explanation is expected. Old Tom Watson, the founder, once said that it's a shame if a healthy salesman works in his territory for a whole year and doesn't achieve his quota.

Similarly, if you are a production supervisor and the plant has been around awhile, you have plenty of historical records to tell you what the normal output should be per hour, per shift, per day, and per week. You also know the quality measures to use, for you have measurable reject rates, rework percentages, and warranty charge-backs from the field.

Most production and sales jobs have ten or twelve standard indicators which the accounting department—especially your cost accountant—is already generating and disseminating to the managers on a regular basis. Even without a formal goal-setting system, you should be using some standards of performance for sales and manufacturing positions. However, it's not so simple to determine what indicators to use in other areas of the organization. Some guidelines for measuring the unmeasurable are provided in chapter 8.

I have studied hundreds of sets of objectives from a wide range of organizations and generally find that with only a little work and a modicum of common sense you can divide the goals by level of organization.

Higher levels of management have mainly financial indicators. The president, group vice presidents, division managers, and profit center managers need to be clear on what their profit targets are in advance of the operating period.

Staff and technical departments have mainly program objectives that identify outputs for a period of time and include statements of cost, quantity, quality, and milestones. (A milestone is the date when the next level of management will review results.)

The lowest management levels have objectives based upon output for a period of time, not upon the variety of activities they perform to produce the output.

A project management system like PERT (Program Evaluation and Review Techniques) or a similar tracking system is used for special areas such as engineering or research and development. These systems are well developed and well documented. There is no mystery about them. Their strengths and weaknesses in practice are well known, and resistance to them is predictable. This resistance comes in the form of grumbling which you must respond to. The critical path method (CPM) is standard for engineering construction projects. You are being buffaloed by the troops if you are managing without it just because people declare that it won't work. It does work, and you can insist that people make commitments to it if you work at implementing it skillfully. You cannot let yourself be put off from defining objectives for the organization simply because somebody has adopted an anti-planning stance and gets loud about it.

You must listen carefully to everything people say when goals are being set and you must adapt the goal-setting process—and the goals themselves—to the realities which the jobholder points out. On the other hand, it's not good management or good human relations to let the organization drift simply because some anti-planners want to wing it at your expense.

People need to be committed to specific outputs for a specific period of time if they expect any countercommitment from the organization, such as a regular paycheck. Teachers must teach, engineers must engineer, and staff people must advise and research, and all must make commitments to do so. How they will do their jobs should be open to discussion up front. The purposes of the organization flow down from the top; methods for getting to those purposes should flow up from the experts.

Ten Common-sense Rules

Having established these necessary conditions, let's look at some of the common-sense elements of the goal-setting process for managers. Unfortunately, common sense isn't really all that common. Thus I suggest the following ten rules:

1. Use indicators and indices wherever they can be used.

2. Use common indicators where the jobs are numerous and alike, and use special indicators for special jobs.

3. Let people participate in devising indicators for their jobs rather than imposing them from the top or having them created by a special staff expert who has never done the job.

4. Never avoid using indicators, but never fully believe the indicators. Some human explanation is needed to make them meaningful.

5. Use past results to create indicators for the future, but not as the only source.

6. Never set an indicator in place without having a reason for it.

7. Be mindful that the indicator or index isn't an end in itself, it's a means of getting where you want the organization to go.

8. Change or dump any indicator that stops action. They should promote action, not stifle it.

9. Get people committed to the indicators by involving them in thinking them up.

10. Always watch for innovative and creative things that fall above and beyond the indicator system, then praise and encourage them.

Goal Setting Requires Trade-offs

Managing by objectives necessarily involves making trade-offs among various objectives. Whenever a manager or a firm sets a goal, at the same time it excludes some other goal. If you put your emphasis upon research and development, you can't spend that same money on something else such as marketing or a new plant. In effect, goals are a choice you make in how you will use your energy.

If you decide to develop a new engineering plan along line A, you may not be able to afford line B. It's true that you may split your efforts by doing half A and half B, but you can't both do something and not do it at the same time. We make trade-offs constantly whenever we set goals.

You can set so many goals that you do a bum job on all of them, or you can have such high standards of perfection that you fail to achieve any of your goals.

As every freshman student of economics knows, economics is the allocation of scarce resources across unlimited demands. This basic rule of economics also fits the goal-setting process. You can't achieve everything in the world, or everything you might think of. You need to make choices among the many trade-offs which are possible. You don't get perfect safety without trading off some production. You don't get harmony and progress all the time. You can't have a perfect quality record when you've also got to be concerned with costs.

Individual versus Organizational Goals

The system of MBO calls for the boss and subordinate to sit down face-to-face and discuss what the objectives of the subordinate's job will be for the coming year. This doesn't suggest that the subordinate has an open checkbook to set any goals that he or she chooses. The boss, too, has some demands and needs which the organization requires, and it is this area of possible disagreement or even confrontation that makes for hard and serious negotiating in the MBO process.

Systems exist and have their own requirements which need to be met, and it is the responsibility of the boss to divide the labor so as to make sure that all of the necessary system requirements are being covered.

Because the subordinate has more experience in his or her own job than anyone else, usually even more than the boss, a listening stage for the boss is a wise and productive aspect of negotiating goals. From time to time the subordinate heartily longs to pursue some pet project which would not allow time for the system to get what it needs. In such cases the boss must persuade, cajole, and finally may have to order that goals be congruent with the system. The point isn't that bosses win or that subordinates win. Rather it's that each enters the negotiation with a listening attitude and a willingness to trade off some personal hobbies or hankerings for the good of the organization.

Trade-offs against Other People

When the boss uses only a one-on-one style of goal setting, the burden of allocating responsibilities among competing people and groups rests squarely in his or her lap. An arbitrator is probably needed when two people think they should be responsible for the same work, the same customers, the same products, the same markets, the same services, or the same people. For one thing, without trade-offs there will be jurisdictional disputes which can occupy all too much time if they are left to be fought out during the year.

The time to settle questions of turf is when goals are being defined and commitments made. Relationships are always a legitimate topic of conversation during the goal-setting session. Empire builders are best handled before they start expanding. Battles over authority are a tough but necessary topic of concern when objectives are being established.

Likewise, the boss must be concerned that all of the required organizational objectives be farmed out to responsible people who will be committed to their achievement. If the boss isn't careful, certain important responsibilities will fall between the cracks. Often these are joint accountabilities which somehow just didn't get discussed in the one-on-one sessions.

Thus it's a sound practice to hold group meetings to share goals among people on the same level. Get everyone in front of the room to present their objectives to their colleagues and to answer questions. You can build teamwork and collaboration right there if you do the group goal sharing well.

Apparent versus Real Effectiveness

A common pitfall for people setting objectives is to play the numbers game exclusively. That is, they hang up some specific numbers as goals rather than try for something which is vastly more important but not as measurable. For example, you might assign X calls per week to the sales force and they might do quite well at beating that number. Their apparent effectiveness is high, but if they're not making sales or getting new customers, their real effectiveness is being traded away in favor of number beating.

It's true that specific goals are easier to understand and pursue if they are quantified, but this can lead to beating an easy number in place of pursuing an important innovation. Lots of people beat the numbers to make their department look good while they are in fact costing the organization money.

Good goal setting centers on measuring real effectiveness— achievement of the overall goals of the organization. The person who concentrates on his or her own personal glory is likely to be a handicap to the team effort. The supervisor who neglects maintenance to break production records looks fine at the moment, but over the long haul the whole plant goes downhill.

Contribution is more important than personal record breaking from the organizational viewpoint. People have to trade off some personal glory for the good of the whole. Good team play should be built into the management system and recognized when it occurs.

Ends versus Means

A few years back, one large electrical manufacturer found itself in the press and on television because its executives had conspired to fix prices. The Justice Department took a dim view of this and a judge slapped giant fines and some jail sentences on the people involved. That firm had a well-oiled and tightly run MBO program. But each executive had been given impossible sales and profit goals, which ultimately led to secret meetings in hotel room with their competitors to fix prices. The executives were sure that without such action they would never make their sales and profit targets. They quite clearly lost sight of the ends versus means trade-off.

Goals are vital, but there are always limitations on the means by which goals can be attained, and these should always be discussed fully and clearly up front when objectives are being set. This will generate some valuable discussion about problems in the subordinate's job of which the boss should be aware.

Long Term versus Short Term

One of the most common complaints about the American management system is that it presses managers to take a short-term view. Goals tend to be set for one-year periods, or for even shorter time spans. The division general manager who misses the quarterly profit goal is an endangered species in his or her own organization.

As a result of the pressure for short-term results, money which could be productively spent in developing new opportunities gets diverted to achieving an immediate gain. This cascades down into the organization so that people in middle- and lower-management positions are strongly discouraged from taking a long-term view of their own jobs and its challenges.

This isn't the fault of the president of the firm. He or she in turn often must face investment analysts for the pension trusts and mutual funds who have only next quarter's profits on their minds. A slight letdown of earnings per share produces a disproportionate collapse of stock prices as the sharks in flannel suits hasten to dump the company's stock.

It is said that the Japanese manager, faced more with debt financing than equity financing, doesn't feel that pressure and can thus invest in the future. This means investment in development, training, and research and engineering, all of which diminish the immediate goals of short-term profit in favor of long-term goals. General Electric is one of only a few U.S. firms to measure managers on the basis of contribution to strategic goals in addition to how well they balance short-term and long-term objectives.

Pressure for short-term profitability waters down the quality of profits. Accounting practices favor LIFO (last in, first out) over FIFO (first in, first out), everything possible is capitalized, and the long-range future of the business is sold for immediate or apparent effectiveness rather than long-term or real gain.

The Trade-off of Ideas

When the boss and subordinate sit down to discuss possible goals for the subordinate's job for the coming year, the most important trade-off comes from swapping ideas. Sometimes this is a trade-off between what the boss thinks is good and what the subordinate holds firmly as being best. The boss has some directives and strategies received from above, and has to get the troops in line and on the march toward achieving those goals. The subordinate may not be overly enthusiastic about the organization's goals and may suggest some alternative strategies.

The art of listening and telling isn't all that simple. The boss thinks the firm should be making Bibles while the subordinate is solidly in favor of collectible erotica. The next scene should be a

hearty give-and-take. In some organizations the professional standards of lower ranks such as engineers and scientists are higher in
terms of quality and excellence than the company could afford, or
than the market could support at commercial prices. This takes
some talking through to arrive at a suitable agreement.

The major commodity being swapped between the parties then
becomes that of ideas and concepts. The notion that all that need
happen in MBO is for the boss to scream more and the subordinate
to scream less is not in tune with what really happens. It is exactly
this negotiating process which is the heart of MBO. Without the
face-to-face discussion, no commitment will follow. The subordinate should be able to say, "Perhaps I fought and lost, but at least
I was heard and my ideas were presented fully before the decision
was made." That represents the biggest trade-off to be made in goal
setting.

Where possible, use disagreements to challenge people to set
innovative goals. There is excitement in innovation. The boss who
lets people work only at routine goals may rob the organization of
the fruit of the innovative energy of its employees. Be sure that you
insist upon at least one big, innovative, noble goal in every job.

Goals Release Energy

Goals often grow out of an attitude called hope. We hope that we
can gain a market share, or we hope we can cut costs. We don't
hope because we have a full bag of evidence to indicate that the
goal we want can be realized. Rather, we find the means because
we hope that we can achieve the goal.

People who have hope for the future usually set high goals based
upon that hope, and then change their behavior to produce the goal.
This means that you don't simply add up what happened in the past
and extrapolate it into the future to get all of your goals. Some of
them have to be based upon hope and the confidence that by hoping
hard enough you will find the resources and the energy to make
them happen.

Small businesses often start out with the idea that something
might be possible. The entrepreneur believes and hopes to make it
happen, even though the money to finance the business may be no-

where in sight. If the idea and the hope are strong enough, the money will appear. There is plenty of venture capital for people who have an idea in which they believe strongly enough.

Lots of goal setting means following a path that actually produces the desired result. We set innovative goals to make things happen. If we make a commitment to that innovative idea, it comes true more often than not. Nothing innovative follows when we don't pursue our hopes.

8

Clear Goals
and Unfailing Feedback

The slovenliness of our language makes it easier for us to have foolish thoughts.

—George Orwell

Any jackass could set an objective for predicting the rising of the sun tomorrow. It has been rising and setting for millennia, and because it has followed an unchanging pattern, it can be predicted. The chances are extremely good that the sun will rise in the east tomorrow, and set in the west. Our level of confidence in this occurrence is very high. Similarly, in certain kinds of occupations it is possible to make predictions and set objectives with a high degree of confidence because we have so much history. If a paper mill turned out 10,000 tons per day all last year, averaged the same for the last half-year and the same for the last quarter-year, it's pretty safe to predict that it will average about the same tonnage per day next quarter as well. Sure, on any particular day it may fall below that, or go higher, but if you have a lot of history you can study that history to learn the probable outcomes for the future.

All of this means that some kinds of goals are much easier to set than others. In the manufacturing plant where things are stable, and no major changes in equipment or product are planned, the results are predictable within a range of variation. Likewise in sales, stability is easier in territories where you have experienced old hands, longtime customers, and unchanging products.

But what about those jobs where the major product is innovation? Where the job incumbent was hired precisely because he or she is creative and innovative? If they innovate, by definition they will produce something that hasn't been seen before, a novelty item or program. How do you set objectives for such people? Indeed, how do you set objectives at all for staff jobs in areas like personnel, employment, training, traffic management, accounting, the law department, engineering, purchasing, data processing, and many others where the output isn't hardware, such as tons or board feet? What if their output is software, made and sold for internal users? The staff department may have only one or two clients, and they are inside the company rather than outside. In many cases, one department's staff work is highly dependent upon the finished work of another department being delivered to them on time and in the right form. Suppose those other turkeys don't do their job. Should I be held responsible?

Two guides which are expanded upon in this chapter will help answer some of these sticky and quite common questions. First, the ideal isn't to produce predictions but commitments on the part of the subordinate; not to forecast the future but to create it. Secondly, commitment doesn't exist if fuzzy goals are produced up front.

Fuzzy Goals Don't Work

Nothing can wreck an MBO plan faster than fuzzy goals.

To understand how to make your goals clear, you must first master the distinction between fuzzy goals and measurable ones. *A fuzzy goal is one that describes inputs or activities: a measurable goal is one that describes specific outputs.*

These three words—inputs, outputs and activities—are the three basic elements in the systems approach. *Inputs* are resources like money, labor, time, materials, and supplies that will be consumed. *Activities* include work, action, processes, and behaviors, any of which may be productive or unproductive. *Outputs* are the products or results, the goods produced and the services rendered. The purpose of goal setting is to define hoped-for output or expected results.

Based upon these definitions, there are two basic rules which apply for making fuzzy goals measurable:

Rule 1: You should always be able to differentiate between inputs, activities, and outputs.

Rule 2: Whenever you see an input stated as a goal ("To spend $100,000 on safety next year") or an activity stated as a goal ("To do our jobs in a safe and effective manner"), insist that the input- or activity-based objective be rewritten as an output statement ("To operate with an accident frequency rate of .5 per million man-hours").

As a simple test, try labeling the following statements as inputs (I), activities (A), or outputs (O):

1. To reduce accident frequencies from .5 to .1 by June 1st.

2. To coordinate the efforts of related departments.

3. To motivate the sales force to improve sales.

4. To start to plan Sunday openings for selected stores.

5. To reduce the customer complaint rate from 4% to 1%.

6. To inspire renewed integrity in expense accounts.

7. To investigate the possible causes of executive burnout.

8. To produce a report on the causes of turnover by May 1st.

9. To prepare an emergency traffic plan by November 1st.

10. To obtain 100 percent participation in the United Fund drive.

You are correct if you marked only 1, 5, 8, 9, and 10 as output statements. All the others describe what you will do, or what will go into the process, not what will come out. Remember that outputs are the end operational results, they are the conditions which will exist if the job is well done or poorly done.

Suppose a subordinate comes to you bearing activity statements—instead of results or output statements—and tries to foist them off as goals. This is when your interviewing and counseling skills come into play. You ask, "And what effect will that have?" over and over until the subordinate becomes specific and states an output. A typical exchange might be as follows:

"My primary objective for the next quarter is to improve pro-ductivity," says the subordinate.

"Please be more specific," says the boss. "What is the present level of productivity, and what level is it that you plan to achieve?"

How to Measure the Unmeasurable

In some instances you may be confronted with a subordinate who would like to define a specific output but who simply doesn't know how to state the objective in measurable terms. Here are some guides for measuring outputs that seem to be unmeasurable:

Can the output be counted? Tons, pounds, feet, dollars, and units are all measures that readily fit most production and sales objectives. Make sure in using these that your goals statement con-sists of (1) a specific output for (2) a specific period of time. For example, thousands of diodes per shift, crankshafts per day, tons per hour, dollar income per month, or lost accounts per quarter.

Can you construct a ratio? Even if the output cannot be counted, you might still be able to measure it by using some ratio. These are particularly useful in staff areas such as traffic, legal, pur-chasing, personnel, public relations, and the like and in nonmanu-facturing organizations where software outputs consist of advice, service, information, and new knowledge. Some sample ratios used in various industries and staff specialties include occupancy rates (a hotel and hospital indicator), complaints to compliments (an airline service indicator), offers to hires (an employment indicator), and credit losses to sales (a sales management indicator).

Can you devise a scale to measure the output? When the results cannot be counted and you cannot construct a ratio for measuring them, you may still be able to devise a scale. For example, you might construct a checklist of housekeeping items and rate yourself on a scale of 1–5 for each item, or you might measure employee attitudes by using a scoring system on opinion surveys. The *New York Times* has developed such a scale for rating the quality of writ-ing in specific stories by its editorial personnel. The standards are spelled out in advance, and the judge is an experienced editor.

Can you use a verb or other action word to make the objectives statement results-centered? When all of the above methods for measuring the output are unworkable, then you must resort to verbs to do the trick. Using words does not mean that nothing is measured. A verb is an action word (for example, "cut," "check," "fix," "buy," "sell") and while it does in fact describe only an activity, that activity in some instances is the result sought. A verb, you see, is a binary word. That is, the result is either 0 or 1. For example, you sold the division (1) or you didn't (0). You performed the credit check (1) or you didn't (0). Did you complete the job? Buy the carload? File the suit? Drill the hole? Hire an engineer? When the objective is to take an action that produces the result sought, you either did it or you didn't, and the result can be stated as either 0 or 1. Admittedly this isn't as good as counting output, looking at a ratio, or measuring results on a scale, but it makes a fuzzy goal measurable.

Can you describe the desired output in words? "To produce clear, readable copy ready for the printer by December 1st" isn't very countable, and what constitutes clear, readable copy is not spelled out. Obviously this is far less precise than the sort of goals produced by the methods described above, but it does present something which is presumably intelligible to both boss and subordinate.

If you are unable to do any of the five things listed above to count, compare, rate, or describe the hoped-for output, my advice to you is to forget the whole thing. Don't spend any more of your time on it because you don't know what you want, and don't spend any other resources trying to achieve it.

Divide Your Goals into Ascending Classes

Another means to sharpen fuzzy goals and make them more measurable is to classify all of your goals into three categories:

Category I: Regular Objectives

These are the ordinary, recurring, ongoing, and routine repetitions of what has happened in the past. In such cases you can pull out last year's results and use past experience as a basis for determining a suitable goal for the future.

The salesman whose sales volume has been $10,000 per month for the past year has a ready reference for setting next year's sales goal.

The production manager who produced an average of 1,000 units per hour over all of last year can be expected to start from that base in choosing a target for the next year.

The employment manager who hired 500 people a month last year can safely project that as a base level for next year.

You don't just copy last year's results. What you do is apply Odiorne's Law ("Things that do not change will remain the same") and use last year's results as a basis for determining next year's goals, unless you realistically expect a specific change.

Category II: Problem-solving Objectives

These goals state a problem in terms of (a) the present condition and (b) the desired condition. The objective is to get from (a) to (b) by a specific time. "To reduce costs from $20 per unit to $15 per unit by May 1st" is an example of a problem-solving objective.

Inspecting this carefully, you will note that it starts with a clear statement of the present condition and then defines where that condition should be if the problem is solved. There are three elements here: *to* alter something *from* a specific position or figure *to* something better.

Every job has problems, and if you can identify them generally, all that remains to make the fuzzy goals measurable is to state the problem in these terms.

Category III: Innovative Objectives

The last category includes objectives that will change things for the better, regardless of how good things may be at present, and even if the present condition does not constitute a problem. Innovative objectives begin with the assumption that anything can be done better, faster, cheaper, easier, safer, more efficiently, or with greater dignity for the people doing the job. Innovative objectives often change the character and direction of the job—or the organization—for the better.

It's not as easy to state innovative objectives in measurable terms as it is for both regular and problem-solving objectives. Yet, with a little thought and effort, specific outputs for innovations can be described. For example: "To introduce zero-base budgeting in the aeronautical division by January 1st" implies a backup program to be followed in innovating with zero-base budgeting. Usually new program innovations call for stages, which should be turned into specific targets and objectives.

Innovative objectives are often conditional. This means that Stage II is conditional upon the successful completion of Stage I, and a specific time commitment is made for completing each stage.

Every manager, from first-level supervisor to CEO, should always have at least one or two innovative objectives on which he or she is working.

These three classes of objectives comprise an ascending scale of excellence. People who do only the ordinary and routine items implicit in their job descriptions contribute less than those who, in addition, see and solve problems. And those who are both routine performers and problem-solvers and who also make improvements in their jobs through planned and committed innovation are the best contributors.

Establish Target Ranges

Even the most exact science includes approximations, so don't press people too hard to give you a single number which they intend to beat. Rather, establish a range of three output levels by asking:

1. What is the most *realistic* level of results? Why do you say that it is realistic? Where did that number come from? How did you devise that rating scale?

2. What is the most *optimistic* figure you can think of? What is the maximum possible in the situation? What would you expect if everything went exactly right? What would your stretch objective be?

3. What is the most *pessimistic* figure you can think of? What

would you consider the lowest permissible or acceptable level of output to be? What would be considered as failure? What would you expect if everything went wrong? At what point would you holler for help by notifying the boss?

Stating the expected output in a range of three estimates is possible with virtually every goals statement. This is what is meant by making goals tough, realistic, and attainable. The top figure becomes the tough goal. The middle figure, based upon what has occurred in the past and modified by new information, is the realistic goal. The range between the top and bottom figures is what is attainable. Like an artillery battery that fires both high and low to "bracket the target," you bracket your realistic goal with control points. This indicates to the subordinate that the boss is realistic and recognizes that not everything can be forecast with precision.

Remember that the purpose of goal-setting is not to forecast the future but to control it, and control is never precise.

Where There's a Will

If people really want to define goals that are clear and measurable rather than fuzzy, they can generally do so, with a little thought. But often they have another reason for wanting to avoid being pinned down. They don't trust the motives of the boss or the organization. They're afraid of setting a trap for themselves. Sometimes the fuzzy goals are put forth exactly because it would be difficult to measure them later on, thus enabling the subordinate to say, "You can't tell whether I actually did what I said I would do because the goals we agreed upon weren't clear. You can neither deny my success nor assert that I failed."

Thus, generating trust between boss and subordinate is perhaps the best starting place for eliminating fuzzy goals. That trust is based upon confidence that the whole goal-setting process is one which benefits both sides. The subordinate will know in advance what is expected. The boss will be able to plan. The subordinate will be free to choose his or her own means to get to the agreed-upon ends. The boss is there to help, not merely to judge. A boss who acts only as a judge, never as a helper, will probably find that people can somehow never think of ways to make their fuzzy goals measurable.

Clear Feedback Follows Clear Goals

Goals alone won't provide self-control. They do add to the organization's control over the subordinate. When the goals have been established and agreed upon, and the subordinate has made a commitment to produce them, the company has gained an important advantage. The tightest and best form of managerial control is having a responsible person committed to the achievement of a company goal, and having that commitment in clear, specific, and tangible form. For the employee, self-control is something else.

Self-control implies that one is moderately, if not completely, free. All behavior is volitional in the sense that all of the bonds that hold us are of our own making. No one, of course, is free to go gallivanting about ripping up other people's rights, persons, property, or sense of well-being.

The control we exert over ourselves, however, is of our own making. The ropes with which we tie ourselves are of our own choice. If I enter a contract, make a promise, pledge an action, or commit to perform openly, I am bound, of course, to comply fully with its terms. To that degree I am bound by others. The freedom to enter into the employment arrangement or not to enter is the area of self-control. Having once entered it, I now have some bonds of obligation. This isn't absolute slavery, for I can leave, and the decision to assume the job was my own to make or reject.

Charles R. MacDonald, longtime executive at ITT, in his book *MBO Can Work!*, describes in some detail the goals and results program at that communications giant. The system there is called Management by Contract. Like a commercial or labor contract, it is entered into by the two parties freely.

The completion of a contract or joint agreement to which both parties are committed doesn't end the transaction. Delivery of specific performance is the meat and potatoes of the contract. The level and quality of the performance is the gist of the agreement, the purpose for the arrangement. Hence the parties should have some means of knowing how completely or adequately they are fulfilling their commitments. In the parlance of behavioral science this is known as feedback, a shorthand word for letting the committed members of the organization know how well their actual performance complies with their commitments to objectives for which they are accountable. To make MBO work, people must be aware of their actual results.

In 1942, at an army camp in South Carolina, I had just finished three months of basic training under a beast of a sergeant. I was hyped up beyond belief at the prospect of a weekend pass. On the long-awaited Friday night when the passes were to be handed out, my group was whistled out into the streets of the camp and rudely informed that all passes were cancelled. We were to work on the rifle range instead, scoring and replacing targets for a visiting team of experts who were practicing for an upcoming national rifle match.

Not thrilled at this honor, we found ourselves in the rifle pits the next day, behind a giant earthworks, pulling and marking targets for the hotshot marksmen, with the temperature climbing toward a hundred degrees. By midafternoon we were in a state of rage and rebellion when one kid from Rutgers suggested we get some revenge by marking the targets wrong. Suddenly the whole activity became joyous. If one of the experts hit the bull's-eye—a common occurrence—he got a fake signal that he had hit the four ring instead. The army's finest marksmen were not getting accurate reports of their results. In one moment of excess, the national rifle champion was greeted with a flag indicating a complete miss of the whole target when in fact he had scored a bull's-eye.

A sudden silence fell over the range. Then, without warning, the entire team of old soldiers raced across the distance from the firing line in a wild charge, dropped into the pits, and began punching out the hapless privates who had played such a dirty trick. No match for the veterans, we were pounded around soundly, and for the next two days we meekly pulled targets and marked them accurately, without fail.

The lesson was clear to every one of us in the pits: Deny a person an accurate knowledge of the results of his or her work and you produce an enraged, frustrated, and rebellious individual. In this case, the recipients of the false reports were able to take direct action against their tormentors, but for many others such an emphatic and satisfactory recourse is denied. Mortgages, pension plans, family responsibilities, career hopes, and a dozen other reasons cause them to swallow their rage, smile through the indignities, and suppress their frustration.

Knowledge of results is a vital and motivating influence upon the behavior of people at work. It affects both their results and their attitudes toward their work. Yet the results themselves are meaningful only if there are clear objectives to begin with. Without a clear understanding that a bull's-eye is the perfect result, and that lesser rings are lesser levels of success, the results are meaningless trivia. The full power of MBO as a managerial system still remains to be fully exploited in most organizations. It requires a full spelling out of goals in great detail, and, equally if not more important, an accurate and immediate knowledge of results.

Eighteen Ways that Goals Improve Motivation

An MBO program is more than a procedure for the personnel department or the salaried personnel records. It's not an addition to anybody's job but a way of doing the job that enhances an organization's motivation. It does this in eighteen ways that I can name:

1. It defines effectiveness as the increase in the value of resources resulting from a person's activities and processes. It means seeking added value at every level of the organization.

2. It recognizes that humans are success-seeking creatures. Nobody goes to work to fail, but they do better work if it's done in the search for success than when it focuses on preventing failure.

3. Life for all of us is lived most fully when it has meaning. Goals are what infuse meaning into work. Without meaning, work is pain and we must be bludgeoned into it.

4. You cannot succeed without a definition of success. Thus

success is only possible if you define goals in advance. You must expect something to produce success.

5. Success in an organization always involves other people on whom you are dependent. This dependence works best if all hands are similarly committed to a better future as defined by job objectives.

6. Your goals always start inside yourself, not in the situation and the environment alone. You must be a decider in order to manage by objectives, not a drifter. Drifters don't need objectives.

7. Success always involves other people. They must collaborate, and so must you. As the poet John Donne said, "No man is an island, entire of itself." If you succeed, it is only worthwhile if your success is recognized by others.

8. Getting in tune with the world means making commitments to others whose opinion is important to you—commitments to generate some specific output by a specific time, when the outcome is in doubt.

9. MBO requires that you think affirmatively about the future, and this produces a kind of affirmative attitude toward work, life, and yourself.

10. Knowledge of results is a powerful force in growing and learning. Take away knowledge of results from human activity and you rob people of motivation and either create zombies or foment a rebellion.

11. Without goals you cannot operate under self-control. It is this self-control aspect of MBO that produces the highest level of motivation. People want to have some power over major portions of their lives, and a well-executed MBO system provides it. Though you are committed to others for results, the means of attaining them are yours to decide.

12. Objectives which are your own responsibility help you identify with the larger organization of which you are a part. If the organization is prestigious and well known because of

its products or is well thought of because of its services, you share in that image if you know your contribution to the organization. Your sense of belonging is enhanced.

13. Achieving goals which you set and to which you commit yourself enhances your sense of adequacy. A banner year, a successful quarter, or the achievement of a lofty goal makes you feel adequate to what others expect of you, and this improves your own self-esteem.

14. If you and others have set goals and are struggling to achieve these goals together, you have a high sense of belonging. This gregariousness is a basic motivator for most people, and the goals are a glue which binds you to the rest of the world.

15. Your security can be internalized if you know what is expected of you and have confidence in your ability to produce what is expected. You don't wonder "Am I doing OK?" Because the standards were spelled out in advance, you can tell exactly how well you are doing in your work while you are doing it.

16. Through goal setting and achievement you can actualize yourself. That is, you can discover what your full capacity is and you can live up to it. You live a half-life at best if you are uncertain, ambiguous, or in conflict with yourself over whether or not you are succeeding.

17. Goal setting creates a sense of power over your own life, especially the part that has to do with your work. You aren't a marionette dangling at the end of another's string, but control much of your own affairs.

18. With goals you can be a winner. Without them you can never win, you can merely avoid loss and avert failure.

Part III
Competence:
The Goal of Training

———————

Life in the jungle is not a status struggle—rather it is the reverse. Animals know their status and the status of all the others in the group. It is the large numbers, the anonymity, the changing forms of organization and the frequent new groupings and relationships which make corporation life so much more anxious and insecure than life in the jungle.

—Anthony Jay

9
Training as a Tool
of Integration

The more incompetent people are, the easier it is to improve their performance.

—Thomas F. Gilbert

Training is a heavy cannon in the armory of an organization's development and human resources specialist. American faith in the values of education has certainly permeated the large corporation. IBM is reported to expend budgets ranging into the billions for the training of its customers and its own employees. According to one report, more than 45,000 full-time equivalent employees were in training at IBM in a recent year. That is, adding the total hours of employee and management training and converting them into forty-hour weeks, the number of IBM employees in training during a year approximates the size of a large university such as Ohio State. Other corporate giants such as the Bell System and General Motors similarly lay out copious budgets for training. The American Society for Training and Development estimates that the total budget for in-company training is nearly equal to the entire education budget of the public schools, colleges, and universities in the United States. This is a tremendous testimony to our faith in training as an instrument of corporate policy.

When times get tough, nonessential business functions are, of course, the first to be eliminated. But during the recent depression of the early eighties, training did not appear to be as severely cut back as some other functions. In earlier years a slight reversal in the budget, sales, or profit picture often produced disastrous cutbacks in training. A good case could be made today that the training and management development function has arrived professionally as an essential contributor to organizational purposes.

Managers Wanted

The creation of formal, planned programs aimed at the development of managerial talent is a relatively recent development, occurring primarily after World War II. During the war years most young
men were in the armed forces and out of the mainstream of man-
power. Senior managers who might otherwise have retired remained
on the job and then retired in exceptionally large numbers during
the years immediately following the end of the war.

In addition to the number of managerial vacancies caused by
the post-war surge in retirements, two further influences created a
high demand for managers. One was the rapid growth of large firms
through mergers, with a steady decline of family capitalism, and
national economic growth. The other was the rising ratio of managers to workers, with the creation of wholly new managerial positions. Senior staff positions in such areas as personnel, labor relations, research and development, traffic, and purchasing were all
added to the managerial complement in typical firms. Because of
the resulting shortage of managers, the idea of management development became a formalized and standard part of the human resources function of most large corporations.

University executive development programs blossomed, tuition
refund plans were installed to allow younger managers to attend
evening degree-granting programs, and association programs for
management development sprung up everywhere. Many firms created their own management development centers where middle
managers were sent to be trained in executive and managerial skills.
General Electric created such a center at Crotonville, New York, in
the fifties, a precursor to numerous similar programs in other firms.
Today hundreds of corporations and government agencies operate
management development programs.

Yet, despite the level and costs of such programs, doubts have
arisen about whether they actually develop managers, and most especially about whether they create star-quality managers. Not all of
the programs are successful. Some in fact have caused problems of
lower morale, increased managerial turnover, undesirable behavior
on the part of participants, and conflict with their superiors when
trainees return to their jobs. In part this is because the architects of
the programs have failed to distinguish between training to improve

present job performance and training to prepare people for higher-level responsibilities in management.

The Goal of Competence

Training is designed to produce some behavior change on the part of the trained. Behavior has been defined as "activity which can be seen or measured." What kinds of behavior does training money hope to earn as a return?

Thomas F. Gilbert in his book *Human Competence: Engineering Worthy Performance* suggests that the "cult of behavior" is neatly divided into three major subcategories. The first is that of *work*, which values the expenditure of human energy on hard work, sacrifice, and self-denial. The second is the subcult of *knowledge*, which values those who have stored up great reservoirs of information, theories, and skills. The third is the subcult of *motivation*, which holds in high regard eagerness and positive mental attitudes on the job. In some ways, this cult of behavior, for which endless amounts of money appear to be available, has some Theory X assumptions. It sees people as requiring training to overcome their inborn negativism of motivation, which produces inability to acquire new knowledge, which is matched by an innate distaste for work.

An alternative outlook toward the purposes and methods of training is, of course, possible under the assumption that management's job is to integrate the member of the organization into the purposes of the organization. In order to successfully sit down with one's boss and discuss how one's personal goals can be shaped to fit the organization's, the subordinate must have a quality called *competence*, or the ability to perform the necessary tasks. If I don't know how to do something it would be foolish of me to make a commitment to do it. This requires that the organization go farther than simply stating its policy to set goals by a dialogue between every boss and every subordinate. The organization must take the next step and provide me with the training that provides the necessary competence. The need to produce an outcome or results creates the need for competence, which is the purpose of training.

Competence isn't a permanent quality, a fixed, lifelong attribute. Rather, as Saul Gellerman put it, competence is more like the hair on a man's head; that which we see today may not be there tomorrow. Training is as much a matter of nourishing the present crop of competence as it is equipping the person for a competence investment that can be used for a lifetime in the service of the employer. Training may in fact be more like a hair transplant that needs a steady infusion of new roots of competence if the declared system of shared goal setting and self-control is to be anything more than a cruel hoax. Two kinds of competencies emerge from the changing world in which we work:

1. We must acquire the competence to do the present job if we are to be integrated into the organization by any method.

2. We must acquire a steady infusion of new competencies to assure future integration.

Motivation and the will to work hard, on the other hand, are hardly a major fruit of training. They grow out of the system of management, the organization culture, the behavior of supervision, and the personal situation of the worker.

How real is the need for ever-increasing infusions of competence? How can this demand be related to the rising levels of human resource obsolescence? There are enough reports about drastic shake-ups in the labor market to suggest that not every employer is really doing a good job of preventing human resource obsolescence, even though they spend copiously for "training."

What Causes Obsolescence?

Even as the pressure to produce engineering graduates for industry and defense positions continues to grow, knowledge workers in American industry and government are being shunted aside and retired in unprecedented rates. The Bell System, for example, has announced that some 10,000 workers, primarily in white-collar occupations, will be offered a generous stipend and package deals to induce them into early retirement this year.

In the banking, insurance, and service industries, thousands of knowledge workers will be eliminated with as little fanfare as possible in the coming years. Their cumulative experience and knowledge will be lost, and at quite a price. The costs of this disinvestment in human capital cannot even be totaled, but in dollars it stretches into the billions.

Given the existing circumstances, in which the useful service of employees with high levels of education and long experience in technical, managerial, and professional jobs no longer pays for itself, there is hardly any alternative to separation. From the economic perspective, the action is defensible. What is less defensible is the past policy and practice that allowed the workers to *become* obsolete and which, if unchanged, will make many of today's most valuable knowledge workers obsolete in only a short time. This is what requires immediate attention.

What are some of the major causes of the slide into obsolescence, and how can we go about preventing it? There are four major causes of obsolescence:

1. Technological change is steady and immutable and leaves professionals behind.

2. Technological change is often accompanied by social and cultural change.

3. Economic worth changes, and the human asset steadily loses value until action must be taken to eliminate it in order to preserve the economic health of the organization.

4. Sometimes the individual declines in personal abilities, energy, or health.

All of these forces can, of course, be alleviated by retraining. Unfortunately, most workers in the United States have been left to their own devices when the time comes for retraining. Although retraining seems, objectively, a better alternative than terminating an employee, few companies have such programs.

That sad state of affairs may be changing. There is apparently a growing interest in retraining manufacturing workers to help them fit into the new service-based economy.

Vocational education, veterans' benefits, and training funds for blue-collar workers have become increasingly available as new state laws are passed to prohibit plant closings, threatening to limit management discretion in closing down obsolete or unsuccessful businesses.

The blue-collar percentage of the work force, now about 20 percent, will probably continue to decline into the 1990s. My own estimates are that less that 10 percent of the work force will be engaged in manufacturing occupations by 1995. Retraining of displaced workers will become a top issue for the decade.

This still leaves unresolved the question of retraining white-collar or knowledge workers, if the problem of the displaced accountant, engineer, actuary, computer programmer, traffic manager, salesman, or scientist is discovered only during an exit interview.

Ten Guides to Excellence in Training

Training is big business in both government and industry. Firms like American Bell, IBM, General Motors, Xerox, and Ford not only have their own training centers for managers and employees; many of them sell training to other firms as well. This new commitment to training is all to the good for professionals in the training field, but it does place a new burden on them to produce results that are worth the price.

How can an executive determine whether his or her organization's trainers are doing the best job possible? Ten guides I have found characterize the most effective training programs and can be used as a checklist to measure excellence in the management of your training department or program.

1. Focus on Behavior

A lot of training, especially that which is rooted in the fifties, is aimed at various forms of personality therapy rather than at changing behavior. Supervisory training that deals with making people trustworthy, loyal, helpful, and so on rather than making them productive, creative, and skilled seems to be aimed more at developing good Boy Scouts than good supervisors.

Much of the change in emphasis in training grew out of the theory of B.F. Skinner and the programmed instruction (PI) movement. Trainers soon discovered that it was not the hardware, the PI test, or the teaching machine that was important about Skinner and his disciples. Rather, what's important is organizing knowledge in a way that it can be taught more effectively by any means. We also picked up the useful definition that "behavior is activity that can be seen or measured."

2. Design Training for Results

When the trainer defines a result to be achieved and then produces that result, training becomes a means toward organizational ends. However, the process is the only thing of interest to the trainer in many programs of the past (and some today).

This distinction between process and result is the major difference between the now-defunct sensitivity training and the new and more useful forms of organization development (OD). Sensitivity training was usually centered on the process, while OD centers upon the result. This distinction also differentiates good sales training from ineffective sales training. The latter all too often focuses upon entertainment, which is a process-centered approach to training.

I'm not denying that training must use processes, but they must be a means to a result, not an end in themselves. The objective is learning, not teaching. Remember, learning means behavior change.

3. Relate Training to Its Context

All too often in the past, training sessions were conducted on a copycat basis. That is, some other organization reported success with a training topic or process, so dozens of others followed suit.

It is as much a technique of sound training to study the context of the organization as it is to conduct a well-executed class or conference. The organizational culture and the managerial climate to which the trainee must return should have some supporting characteristics. If the organization cannot support the behavior which training presents, then the training will fail.

4. Identify Training Needs

Not all management problems are behavioral problems. Neverthe-less, the ancient belief that education is a solution to all problems has often been carried over into industrial and administrative train-ing, with some unfortunate effects.

Training professionals need to ask: "Is there really a problem, and is it caused by a lack of knowledge or a shortage of skills, or is it the result of something else, such as bad organization, weak pol-icy, or simply irresolute supervision?"

If the latter is true, training is not prescribed. The system which creates the problem must be worked on first. Policies must be al-tered, or the irresolute supervision must be beefed up or removed. Professional trainers need to learn to say no when people rush into their office requesting a training solution to a problem which is pat-ently not a training problem.

Because behavior change may require changes in the systems by which the organization is operated, trainers need access to the top management of the unit being changed.

5. Identify Training Objectives and Criteria

Before training begins, the objective of the training should be pre-pared, approved, and promulgated. "As a result of attending this training session . . ." should preface every announcement, invita-tion, or course description. The announcement gives management full knowledge of what it is buying, it lets people attending know what they are in for and whether they are attending the right pro-gram, and it helps teams of instructors match their efforts toward a common purpose. The objective comprises the best yardstick for the evaluation of training after its completion.

Stating the objective in simple terms is a fair start, but the ob-jectives should then be clarified, expanded, and made explicit by statements of criteria.

Criteria for training could be examples of the behavior which would indicate the successful completion of the training. Criteria might also include statistical changes in outcomes on the job which would be evidence of behavior change (although this isn't always practical). Criteria might also be ratio changes which should be produced by training, such as the ratio of complaints to compliments from customers anticipated through an employee customer relations training program. Still another type of criteria could be a "go/no-go" or an "if . . . then" statement. The weakest form of criteria is that which consists of adjectives, such as trustworthy, loyal, helpful, and the like, for their meaning is often ambiguous within the training context.

Good training criteria must include a statement of the present condition as well as the desired condition. Without a definition of the present behavior, training may boast achievements which existed before the training took place. Therefore, criteria for training should include a statement of a "from/to" character.

One important criteria for training is that it be innovative. Problem-solving merely restores normality, but the training professional seeks to be an agent of change and betterment.

A good rule for identifying training criteria is to "measure the measurable, describe the describable, and eliminate all the rest."

6. Use Simulation in Training

If I had to choose a single important breakthrough in training as a means of changing behavior, I would choose simulation training. The merit of such methods as role play, management games, case studies, family group OD sessions, incident processes, and the like is not in their novelty or entertainment value but in their demonstrated ability to produce relevant behavior change. The relevance lies in the closeness of the simulated behavior to the actual behavior demanded on the job.

Preparing training that simulates reality is hard work. It requires trainers to get out into the plant, field, or office where real things happen, and it requires that they resist unnecessary prattling about theories which interest them but which are of little benefit to the trainee.

Rather than talking about the motivation theories of Herzberg, McGregor, and Likert, trainers might better spend their time in simulating the behavior which is expected of people on the job, applying those theories in action. Most motivation training does more talking about motivation than teaching managers how to behave in a way that will change motivational behavior on the job.

7. Identify Training Stages

One of the more effective training techniques of the past fifty years was job instruction training (JIT). It was applied in wartime with fantastic success to train millions of unskilled people for wartime industry. A four-step process, JIT insisted that each job being taught be broken down into detailed stages, allowing the trainers to check their own progress and that of the trainees at every step.

Modern adaptations of that approach apply this logic to new training problems. The major advantage of task breakdown, prior to conducting the training, lies in the ability of the trainer to teach for mastery of the competencies sought. If the trainee hasn't acquired the behaviors for a particular step, he or she can then be put through that step again until mastery is achieved.

8. Use Action Training Techniques

Passive behavior by the learner may result in some learning, but if every trainee is required to engage in some kind of action, there is an opportunity for feedback which can reinforce the desired kind of behavior. This is obviously more feasible and useful if the behavior taught is related to the actual environment or system in which it must be performed back on the job.

The feedback may come in many forms, as in a flight simulator where the pilot sees himself crash with his plane if he makes a serious error on landing. Usually the simulation is one in which situational facts resemble but do not fully duplicate the features of reality. However, the trainee's behavior should be a reasonably close enactment of how he or she would behave in the real-world situation. Usually it is better to use action training simulations that demonstrate successful behavior rather than unsuccessful.

9. Provide Feedback

One of the most important aspects of training is that the trainees get feedback on the effects of their actions while that action is going on. Some trainers, especially the behavior-model theorists, believe that the pure act of learning takes place when the feedback occurs.

According to the hot-stove principle of learning, the cat that jumps on a hot stove will never do so again. This is a demonstration of feedback in its purest form. Yet many cats will be required to learn to jump onto cold stoves on the job, to avoid the hot ones, and to discriminate correctly between a hot stove and a cold one in advance of the jump.

Three guides to successful feedback in training might be helpful here:

a. Fast feedback is more effective than slow feedback. The closer feedback comes to being simultaneous with the behavior, the greater the learning effect.

b. Relating the feedback to the behavior explicitly increases the learning effect.

c. Favorable or pleasant feedback will have a better effect than punishing or negative feedback. The pleasing feedback issued for the desired behavior produces that behavior and fosters a desire for more learning. Punishing feedback may extinguish undesired behavior but it may also produce some unintended side effects, including a burning desire to get out of the training situation immediately and to keep away from it in the future.

Behavior modification is largely based upon feedback, and this has attracted a great deal of severe criticism, especially when feedback is applied in a strong negative fashion. The effective use of feedback can change behavior, an awesome fact that places the trainer in a position of playing God with other human beings. As long as training was a harmless and usually ineffective activity, nobody got excited. But now that training has a proven record of changing behavior, it is receiving closer attention for its moral and social consequences.

10. Measure Results Against Goals

The evaluation of training is a much-discussed and often overly confused topic. The problem seems to be finding criteria against which to measure the training effort and expense. Rating the course against participant opinion, top management impressions, and similar measures misses the main point. Training should change behavior that is relevant to the job environment. That behavioral definition should have been clarified in advance, with criteria spelled out, small steps defined in a job breakdown, and those steps simulated in the training.

Trainees can rate the popularity of a program and this will have some political effects on the image of training in the organization. It can also affect future course enrollments. But it cannot determine whether the training was effective. That can only be done by pulling out the original statements of objectives and weighing the new behavior against the old behavior and the objectives. If the objective was mastery, then the extent of mastery comprises the extent of course success.

The continual upgrading of the training profession lies in the development of more hard technologies of training. These are clearly more sophisticated than in the past, and they have a much better track record of doing what they purport to do. The trainer who can change behavior is increasingly seen as an important contributor to the operation and strategy of the organization.

Get More for Your Training Dollar

The price of outside courses is up, the costs of housing people in hotels while attending conferences is hovering at $90 a day in most cities, and air fares are up in the jet stream level along with the planes.

In-house courses are thus becoming more popular because they are more economical. They are also advantageous because you can control what happens and can fit the training to the problems of the organization. In addition, you get maximum mileage from the time of the people involved. This, of course, is the biggest part of the cost, even though such costs are usually concealed, not being directly charged to training.

Here are eleven ways you can maximize the yield from your training dollars:

1. Plan to do more of your training in-house rather than sending people to outside courses, doing the latter only for a specific and specialized course that you cannot handle.

2. Start identifying training objectives for more than a single year. You can't expect to maximize the investment in human resources in a single year.

3. Tie training plans to your organization's strategies. If you're in a growth-centered company, train for growth. If your company is in a maintain-and-harvest mode, train for administrative skill.

4. Be sure every course is run past top management before you invest in it. If the top executives don't endorse, approve, and support the training, you may be sending people to learn things that cannot be supported by the real world in which they work. Try out every new course on a trial group of top managers, and then revise it as they recommend.

5. Make accurate and complete descriptions of training costs, including all out-of-pocket salaries and fees, plus the costs of the time people spend in training. Don't try to do a cheap job. If the objective is really worthwhile, the most expensive training will be that which tries to do it too cheaply. Go top-drawer in quality and save money.

6. Do a precise task analysis of each training need for every program before you offer it. If it is going to work, it must be aimed at real behavior change needs of the organization, not a copycat program from somebody else.

7. Avoid fads. Just because everyone else at the local training directors' association is offering Zen therapy doesn't mean your people need it.

8. Use line managers as trainers as much as possible. Use the training staff, which should be lean, as organizers, trainers of trainers, and strategists rather than just as classroom teachers.

9. Charge costs back to the using units where possible. If the programs are meeting needs, fees for people coming to courses should be paid by the line departments or staff departments sending the trainees. Use the income from such fees to support further training.

10. Make sure the physical environment is adequate. A decent set of training rooms with ample visual aids, library facilities, and

support personnel is an excellent investment for making the rest of your costs pay off.

11. Evaluate every session and every course. Don't just check participant reactions to the course, but sample the changed behavior back on the job on a regular basis. Survey the bosses of the people who complete the training for evidence of application and behavior-change as well.

Maximizing Gains from Outside Training

As the cost of management training continues to rise, the need to improve its payoff also rises. My own estimate is that more than 200,000 U.S. managers now attend some kind of executive seminar or course each year. But while inflation seems to be moderating in the costs of most things, the costs of management training seem to be climbing steadily. One reason for this is that the salaries of trainers and trainees are higher, and both must be calculated in the true costs of training. Sending an executive to the Stanford executive course costs the company $14,000 for the registration fee alone. With the average salary of such participants running upward of $1,500 per week, you've got to add around $12,000 more, plus travel costs and the expense of covering the executive's position while he or she is away, to arrive at the total cost of the training. "Executive MBA" programs now offered by many universities may prove less costly because the executive must donate some of his or her own time in the Saturday portions of the course, but they are still extremely costly.

Most of these eight-week executive courses and two-year executive MBA programs are abbreviated versions of an academic MBA offered to younger people in regular degree-granting graduate schools of business. They teach accounting, finance, marketing, and strategic planning, along with a smattering of quantitative methods. Some include a week or two on international business and perhaps on the social and cultural environment of business.

There can be no doubt that the MBA degree is the major management development program in this country—and many others— today. Perhaps the most important reason for its success is that it deals with the things an executive needs to know about the major functions of a business: marketing, finance, accounting, personnel and human resources, and external relations. In addition it has a strong bias toward policy and strategic planning. Most MBA programs today have a heavy mathematical component, and this gives engineers and science majors attending them an advantage. Even though most companies don't rely too heavily on operations research and quantitative analysis, statistics is one of the major languages of business and most MBAs have a solid grounding in "stat." The case method, started first at Harvard, is now widely used and gives the curriculum a touch of reality which more theory-centered courses of study don't have.

There were only 5,000 MBAs graduated in 1953 when I received my MBA from New York University, and almost half of those were from just four universities. This year more than 65,000 MBAs will be graduating, from nearly every college in the country. Despite cries that the market is flooded, the end is not in sight. MBAs, when they reach the top, insist on hiring more MBAs, in part because they know what the degree consists of, the common language which MBAs speak, and the strong credentials they had to bring to the college admissions office. Admittedly there are two tiers of the MBA degree: one from the major universities (such as Harvard, Penn, Michigan, Columbia, and Stanford) and the other from schools that have jumped aboard the MBA bandwagon to pay the bills of their faltering general education and liberal arts programs.

In addition to the MBA degrees, including the watered-down versions offered in executive programs at various universities, there are some winners in the noncredit sector which are doing a pretty fair job of teaching specialists to become generalists in management:

The American Management Association's management course is a four-week program, spaced out over several months, which must be completed in one year. It runs about 48 weeks a year, and is filled to capacity almost every time.

In every state university from Florida to Washington and from Boston to San Diego, "executive courses" which stress managerial skills are turning out graduates.

Trade and professional associations also offer specially tailored courses for their own industry's management. The American Bankers Association's Stonier School at Rutgers, for example, is one of the oldest and largest. Each year more than 1,200 bank officers attend courses which include heavy shots of banking and strong doses of management.

In the area of human resources, seminars which incorporate team building or variations of interpersonal skills building are a sizable chunk of the management development market. The granddaddy of such course is that conducted at Bethel, Maine, by the National Training Labs. The faculty is made up mainly of professors of education, organization behavior, and psychology. Although once roundly criticized, the program has been fine-tuned into a more practice-oriented interpersonal skills offering today.

Despite all of the growth in the offerings of universities, associations, and consulting firms, there isn't much evidence that such training produces any useful behavior change, and much of that which does result isn't very durable. The fact is that we still accept management training on faith in far more cases than you would imagine from reading the promotional literature of the sponsors.

The first step in getting maximum value from an outside course takes place before you decide to send your people to the course. Not only should line managers be included with the management development staff in deciding who to send; they should also review the advertised content of the course.

Once people are attending a course, someone in high places should plan to visit them. If the president doesn't go, then at least the management development manager should, to spend a day with his or her people and get a feel for what is going on in the program. Almost all university courses welcome such visits, and some even require a boss to spend a day or two with his or her company's participants near the end of the course.

The idea is that you don't want to send people to courses where they learn some skills and acquire some attitudes that can't survive a return to the job. People who attend a course in which they learn how to use participative management and who then return to a hard-nosed, "lean-and-mean" type of organization which doesn't support such behavior would be better off not going at all. If your organization doesn't intend to let people apply what they have learned at the course, don't send them in the first place.

Management training should change behavior through instruction, demonstration, practice, or planned experience. If you can't accept the new behavior which the particular course aims at producing, try something else.

Improving In-House Training

Similar kinds of assessment are vital for in-house programs. The fact that a course has been run successfully elsewhere may or may not be relevant for your organization. There is an important first step in initiating a training course for your people, and that is analyzing the real need for the training. Here's how:

First ask if there is a problem worth solving. If not, forget it; otherwise go on to the next question.

Second, find out if the problem is behavioral or some other kind of problem. If it's a problem of supervision, get the supervisors to do their job. If it's a system problem, change the system. But if it's a behavior problem and you know whose behavior needs changing, proceed to the next step.

Third, describe the present behavior and the desired behavior in very specific terms, remembering that behavior is activity that you can see or measure. If you can't see it or measure it, it isn't behavior.

Improving present job performance should be the objective of most in-house training courses, not preparing people for advancement. The course may be as specific as training salespeople to ask for orders, training supervisors to delegate, or training staff people to conduct effective meetings. The more specifically a course relates to required job behavior, the greater the payoff. Training which "exposes" people to new ideas has a very poor payoff.

Organizing an In-House Training Program

Having pinpointed a real training need, as opposed to a pseudo-training problem, you are ready to organize your program. Here are six steps to follow:

1. Define the end behavior you want to see when the training is completed. State some specific examples of the incorrect present behavior and then give some specific examples of how things will be if people are behaving correctly.

2. Break the training down into small sequential steps. Don't try to solve the whole problem with a one-shot blast of words. Define some specific stages, remembering that training should show and tell people slowly and patiently, one step at a time, until you know that they understand the sought-after behavior.

3. Arrange to have trainees engage in some kind of action in the training process—simulations, games, role playing, case studies, and problems to be solved which resemble the actual work environment to which they will return. Practice and repetition are necessary parts of the learning process.

4. Use feedback throughout the training program so that people will know when they are doing things right and when they're doing them wrong. Don't save the feedback for the end of the course.

5. Follow up after the training to see if people have applied the newly acquired behavior back on the job.

6. Enlist the trainee's boss in converting course learning to on-the-job behavior. Be sure that the trainee's boss knows what was taught, and solicit his or her help as supervisor of the newly trained employee to encourage application of the new skills, or at least to avoid extinguishing what was learned.

Motivation and intelligence are sufficient for purely conceptual learning, but on-the-job reinforcement is required in order to effect a transfer of the classroom behavior back to the job.

In addition to formal training classes, a comprehensive management development program involves coaching, understudy assignments, job rotation, selected reading, planned experience, and performance appraisals.

Engaging Outside Speakers

There is no shortage of well-known people who will gladly come to your meetings and deliver their favorite lecture or seminar for fees upward of $10,000. Even a run-of-the-mill speaker with good credentials and a pleasing platform manner charges about $2,000 per appearance these days. One former electrical company executive who delivers a powerful talk on strategic planning sends back a curt printed form—"Sorry, my minimum fee is $5,000 per appearance"—to those who send him invitations proposing something less.

There is no doubt that big names draw big crowds of registrants to large conventions at fancy fees. A conference which attracts a thousand registrants at $500 per head is a nifty half-million-dollar package. A roster of star-quality speakers is an absolute must for such gatherings. If they have something to say and can say it with style, their high fees may be a bargain. When you have a small group with only twenty or thirty executives, however, the payoff for having such costly speakers is largely to be found in the golden touch which it lends to the conference, flattering the egos of the participants.

Moving down to the less elevated ranks where middle-management and supervisory training sessions are offered, the prices drop considerably, and the rules of the road in hiring outside speakers also change. Here are some guidelines which are most useful:

1. Define a specific training need and communicate that need to the speaker, asking him or her to submit an outline of the presentation to be made which you can review for suitability.

2. Check out the speaker's track record with similar groups, asking for the names of several recent groups addressed. Call the people who ran those programs to request a candid assessment.

3. Make sure that the speaker knows the nature and size of the group to be trained, including job titles, ages, educational levels, and prior training.

4. Don't be bashful about asking past sponsors what they paid the person, and make your offer in the same range.

5. Send a specific letter of intent in which you state your expectations in terms of objectives, starting and stopping times, and any other plans you might have for the speaker's session, as well as the amount and terms of payment (usually a flat fee plus travel expenses).

6. Always distribute some sort of evaluation form after each session to find out how well the presentation was received in terms of usefulness and interest. Among other things, this will protect you from unwarranted criticism from the isolated executive who didn't like the speaker or the message when everyone else loved them both.

10
Management Development to Improve Present Performance

People don't do things for zillions of the darndest reasons, leading to all sorts of problems.

—Robert Mager and Peter Pipe

B efore you start training managers to manage better it would be a pretty sound idea to dig into the behavior you are now getting to find out if it really is a training problem. There are a host of reasons why managers don't manage in the most effective fashion. Perhaps it is because the manager lacks the competence to do the job the way it needs to be done. A lack of skill in interviewing, listening, and communicating, for example, could create the very strong, though erroneous, impression that the offending manager lacked the developmental attitude to produce the best efforts from his people. Such a lack of skill and competence is probably an indication that training will help.

On the other hand, there may be a number of other explanations which are more important than lack of competence. Perhaps the manager knows how to do things right but finds that system obstacles make it unrewarding to follow the right behavior. The training of the past was okay, but its transfer back to the job was not encouraged and may even be punished by red tape, a hostile boss, critical peers, or other behavior snuffers. If the job itself snuffs effective behavior, further training in skills won't do the trick. Only a change in the system, supervision, or rewards structure will produce a change in behavior.

Not only are these immediate job-related system forces likely to produce the wrong kinds of behavior, but there are also changes in the general climate—in the world outside—which make obsolete the kinds of managerial skills which worked in the past. Take the

case of the supervisor or manager who worked his or her way up
through the ranks, starting as a college grad trainee back in 1959.
The very things that worked then and persuaded higher management that this one was a rising star in the organization will now be
the cause of failure. Managers who can't meet the needs of today
because they can't relate to the new work force won't perform well.

Quantitative Changes in Human Resources

A report by the U.S. Department of Labor in December 1979 laid
out a rather clear view of what changes in the shape of the labor
force to expect by 1990. To name a few of the more important ones:

1. White-collar jobs will be up 24 percent, which means that
the existing ratio of white-collars to blue-collars will increase. The
rising cost of labor will accelerate automation, robotics, and the
substitution of machines and devices for laborers. As labor costs
rise to the range of an average salary of $20,000 a year for an av-
erage employee, it will become increasingly economical to replace
people with capital equipment. It will also become easier to substitute foreign labor—through imported products—and to operate in
such foreign locations as Taiwan, Korea, and Mexico.

The future for plant supervision and skilled occupations isn't as
gloomy, because more skilled people such as machinists, technicians, carpenters, electricians, and electronics experts will be required to keep the new automated plants running. Labor relations
as a profession won't grow in factories as fast as in white-collar and
office occupations, and many supervisors in such work sites won't
be ready unless they are trained in labor–management relations.

2. White-collar occupations are most likely going to be filled
with the "baby boomers" who were growing up in the 1960s and
1970s. Because these people have higher expectations than did previous incumbents, participative management and motivational
problems will take precedence over the old-style leadership of hard-
nosed supervision even more rapidly than in the past.

3. The total size of the work force will rise from 98 million to
114 million workers by 1990, which is actually a lower growth rate
than occurred during the 1970s. Service industries will rise to 16.1

million workers, an increase of 30 percent. This will create some tough problems in productivity, for gains in service industry productivity call for different methods of attack than do those in factory- or distribution-based industry. Productivity training will become a hot item during the 1980s, and some innovative ideas would be welcomed in most service organizations.

4. Even with the higher age of retirement under the Age Discrimination in Employment Act, there will be 47 million replacement jobs for workers who die or retire during the decade. Getting new workers in place and ready to work, and upgrading them for higher levels of responsibility will produce some gigantic training problems.

5. More people will be working for large corporations, and there will be fewer self-employed people during the decade. Small companies are gobbled up by larger ones as concentration of industry continues despite periodic bursts of antitrust activity on the part of government. The trend will be especially marked in retail and distribution, where chains are taking over small hot-dog stands, department stores are taking over specialty shops, and nationally franchised businesses are replacing individual shops.

6. More professional managers will be required, and they will be called upon to do things that supervisors ten years ago were never called upon to do. A lot of this will occur because of qualitative changes in the work force, plus new laws and the changing nature of the work force. Blue-collar jobs will decline during the decade, and the model manager will be directing more clerical, technical, and managerial staffs of workers.

Qualitative Changes in the Work Force

Even more important will be the changes in character and expectations of the work force by 1990. Current census results are still incompletely analyzed, but some important changes that will affect the character and direction of training can be seen.

There is already a significant increase in the number of blacks in colleges of business and engineering; they entered the work force in 1982 and their number will continue to grow rapidly. Black students enrolled in colleges of business rose from 41,000 to 221,000 between 1970 and 1978, with comparable figures for engineering and medicine. In 1985 there were a million blacks in college, up from 282,000 in 1970. This population will not only diminish the number living at lower socioeconomic levels, but will also bring people with higher expectation for upward mobility into the work force, expectations that must be dealt with.

The number of women entering business schools has leaped as well and will continue to do so through 1990. Not only are more women in college (4.71 million in 1985, up from 2.8 million in 1970), but they have abandoned the field of education as a career goal. Enrollments of women in business schools have risen from 204,000 to 819,000 and will rise even more rapidly. Up to 60 percent of the applications in some business schools are now from women.

Furthermore, deans and admission directors report that women are winning a disproportionate number of the top academic-achievement spots in business colleges. This, too, will alter what is needed in induction, training, and management development during the decade of the 1980s. The pressures that these good students will exert upon the labor market for opportunities and challenges will be irrepressible. Among the opportunities demanded will be equal training in prestigious in-house company programs and assignments to executive-development programs.

The changes in the environment which are listed above didn't burst upon the scene in an instant. Many firms have proved that it is possible to train managers to accommodate to change, to master new laws and their requirements, deal with different racial and gender groups with different values and strengths. The company cannot reverse the demographic and qualitative changes which are occurring. It can, however, use management development to train managers in the skills of adaptation to these different groups, different labor markets, and new classes of employees.

Four Categories of Managers

Individual differences within the ranks of the management team must also be recognized. There are people who do a good job, and those who don't. There are those who have demonstrated a capacity to adapt, and those who haven't. The first stage of manager development to improve present job performance, then, is to clearly identify the present performance and potential of each manager. Breaking the team into categories according to a mixture of performance and potential creates a kind of portfolio of human assets on the management team. Manager development means taking actions which will enhance the overall value of the portfolio.

Most firms have diversified portfolio of managerial people who might be classified into these four categories:

1. The workhorses, who do a good job but who aren't promotable.

2. The stars, who do a superior job and have lots of potential for advancement.

3. The problem children, who have lots of potential but who aren't fulfilling that potential in their present jobs.

4. The deadwood, who have low potential and who aren't even doing a good job in their present position.

Most supervisors will fall into the workhorse category—people who do a great job at their present post but who, for a variety of reasons, probably won't get another promotion, or at least not more than one. Yet it would be absolutely foolish to think that because these people don't have the star quality that could carry them to the heights, they shouldn't receive training in how to do their own managerial jobs better. At the same time, however, the training strategy for such a population should be tailored to improving their present performance and not something else.

A few years ago one large firm conducted an opinion survey of its employees which included questions relating to attitudes toward opportunities and higher levels of responsibility. They found, to the chagrin of the management development staff, that more than 90 percent of the managers and supervisors indicated that they both desired and expected to be promoted in the very near future. A cursory survey of the growth prospects within the firm made it readily apparent that no such promotions were even remotely possible. It might reasonably be predicted that higher-level jobs could be offered to about 10 or 15 percent of the management team over the next five years, but certainly nothing close to the level of expectations which the survey revealed. A high degree of disappointment was thus predictable among those whose expectations had somehow been raised.

Further study showed that this disparity between reality and expectation had been caused by a vigorously executed management development program which had stated clearly and unequivocally that one of its primary objectives was "to prepare you for higher-level responsibility in the future growth of the corporation." The course designers had aimed at producing something which the organization could never deliver. And since the course had been conducted with considerable skill and imagination, it had quite effectively accomplished something which it should never have attempted in the first place. Every manager—every workhorse, star, problem child, and deadwood—was treated alike, raising the hopes of all.

The lesson to be learned here is that if the course objectives had been shaped from a portfolio analysis of the four classes of managers, this lamentable situation might have been avoided. This story also establishes a principle for management development: Different training objectives for development should be framed for each separate category of people.

> The great bulk of managers will most likely fall into the workhorse category and their training should aim at improvement of job performance in the present position or a position on a comparable level of responsibility. The training given to workhorses should not raise aspirations which cannot be fulfilled.
>
> Management development for stars should be aimed at increasing and developing their high potential for positions and responsibilities that will exist in the future but that may not even be evident today.
>
> Management development for those classified as problem children should be remedial in scope and purpose, aimed at the

personal or situational factors that prevent them from fulfilling their high potential.

Time and effort spent on management development for people who have been soundly identified as deadwood are fruitless and wasteful. It probably even does more harm than good.

How the firm in the story above actually worked its way out of the dilemma which it created for itself is not the major point here, of course. They did in fact make many lateral job moves, introduced some title changes (such as labeling foremen as managers without actually changing their duties), and lost only a small number of people whom they might have wished to retain. The entire exercise was costly, troublesome, and disruptive to organizational efficiency, and might easily have been avoided.

Training Workhorse Employees

One of the clear conclusions which emerges from this case, in the view of professional management development experts, is that the greatest volume of development courses, seminars, and other planned training efforts should aim at improving the performance of most participants in their present jobs. The idea is to aim mainly at improving the skills, behaviors, and attitudes of people so that they can do an even better job on their present assignments. It is not to enhance their promotability by some fancied scheme of creating stars out of people who have shown little if any potential for higher levels of responsibility.

Given such objectives, it is possible to use management development to achieve behavior changes, to add to people's knowledge and skills, to widen their knowledge of the organization and its functions, to improve them in new areas which will raise their value as human assets, and to provide them with more job satisfaction and success. At the same time you can keep doors open to permit the few workhorses whose potential upgrades itself (the "late bloomers") to move into the star category if such a transformation should occur.

New developments in learning theory, training methods, and

behavior modification which evolved during the sixties and seventies are being applied by training and management development departments in the best-run organizations. In large part this has been a result of emerging professionalism in industrial and organizational training applied to improving the job performance of workhorses on their present jobs.

The Challenge of Change

The most compelling reason for training people who lack high promotability lies in the presence of change in the organization. Today's workhorse who is doing a perfectly fine job may become obsolete because of changes in the technology of the work being done. In effect, people can turn from solid performers into deadwood through no fault of their own. Constant and unremitting training is needed to keep people from becoming obsolete.

> The office supervisor in charge of the typing pool needs training in the new technologies of word processing and data processing to avoid obsolescence.

> The accountant who isn't trained in computerized MIS systems will be deadwood in a few years, and such training is even more important—a lot more important—for the supervising accountant.

> The engineering manager who takes no technical and professional retreading courses will likely become a problem child in a short period of time as new technologies and production methods emerge. New products demand new skills, as do new markets, new customers, and new employees.

> The supervisor who hasn't been given training which makes change easy and necessary will become a problem child or deadwood. The fault is not that of the supervisor, but of the employer. The changing values of younger employees make supervision different today from what it was when many old-time supervisors were appointed.

For the eighties and nineties then, the strategy of training which should comprise the core of the management development effort should be meeting the challenge of change. Eastman Kodak's international division has a course aimed specifically at producing change-creating management, and in most high-tech businesses training is the major strategy for remaining competitive in a rapidly changing world. Even in more stable businesses, people must be trained to live with change.

Make Workhorses Comfortable

God must have loved the workhorses because he made so many of them. A study that I recently completed with several large firms to classify people into the four categories showed that approximately four out of every five employees belong to this group. These are the typists, salesclerks, machine operators, bank tellers, machinists, pipe fitters, carpenters, electricians, riggers, truck drivers, janitors, and occasionally first-line supervisors who rose from the ranks.

Workhorses aren't likely to be promoted from their present positions to higher ones. They may have educational limitations (a college degree is often required for higher level positions), or they may be lacking in some technical know-how, special qualities, or particular talents required for advancement.

Workhorses excel at their jobs, enjoy what they are doing for the most part, and make the wheels of industry and government turn. Their importance can hardly be overstated. For this reason, I have attempted to assemble some guidelines for managing these good folk, drawing upon Abraham Maslow's theory for motivation.

Maslow declared that all people have certain needs which must be fulfilled, and which, when unmet, are motivators. Workhorse people have such needs which must be met by their employers and by the jobs they hold. They must have their physical needs met by adequate pay and physical emoluments, they need personal safety on the job, and they need to have a feeling of belonging to something important. They also must have their self-esteem and ego needs met by the work they do and by the way they are managed. Then, in addition, they need to actualize their best capacities. Since, in the judgment of management, these people have little potential for promotion to higher levels of responsibility, all of these needs must be met on the present job.

To me this suggests that we need to design our systems realistically for managing workhorses so as to make such employees comfortable in their present jobs. *Comfortable* in this case doesn't mean that they will be resting or taking it easy, but rather that they are free from the anxieties that come from denial of their basic physical, security, ego, social, and self-actualization needs.

Employers need for their employees to be productive and to make a maximum contribution over the longest possible stretch of time. In managing workhorses to meet this need it is exactly this sense of being comfortable which presents the biggest challenge to an employer.

The strength of the contribution of the workhorse lies in his or her steadiness and self-discipline. Even though a workhorse will never rise rapidly like a young star, and will never be as flashy and mercurial as a problem child, he or she is the prime source of productivity for the organization. A workhorse finds satisfaction in the work itself, not in the possibility of rising. The thrill of ascent to the heights isn't on the agenda. A workhorse will seldom if ever become excited by battling the government in a giant antitrust suit; the winning or losing of great strategic battles is limited to those few who reside in the upper echelon of management. Workhorses will make no sweeping career decisions nor conduct raids on other firms, betting billions on their daring and financial wizardry. But their cumulative value to an employer is beyond estimation, for without them the wheels of the organization would grind to a halt.

As John Gardner said, "We need excellence at every level; in our plumbers as well as our theorists, lest neither our pipes nor our theories hold water." The skilled workman at every level is worthy of his or her hire, and the workman's achievements are honorable and must be treated as valuable by the employer.

If we run our businesses, hospitals, schools, and government agencies in such a way that only the top brass and the rising stars destined for senior positions get satisfaction and pleasure from work, we cripple the organization. The star may never attain stardom if management disregards the workhorses who do the myriad chores that make up the great mass of jobs in the organization.

In managing workhorses, the best approach lies in policies and practices which play upon the workhorse's strengths, stability, loyalty to the organization, and pride in doing a job well. The major strengths of workhorses lie in their competence, and in their satisfaction in the learning of skills and applying them unfailingly and without mistakes.

For some managers, motivation means stirring up the employees to new heights of frenzy. It often means a locker-room speech which sends the passive and torpid ranks of lesser souls forth to win the next commercial game for the Gipper or for the stockholders. In the process they may simply be afflicting people who are comfortable and whose comfort lies in the knowledge that they are competent, steadfast, and reliable.

When this affliction comes down upon them, the employees may actually get worse in their performance, for such exhortations—along with the execution of lean-and-mean tactics—don't improve results, they diminish them. The use of managerial intervention that destroys feelings of competence, recognition, belonging, security, and a sense of adequacy and self-esteem should only be undertaken in the most draconian of circumstances.

When ordinary workers are doing what is expected of them and doing it well, it is foolish to demand radical changes and impossible levels of performance when the only imaginable purpose is to ease the stress and anxiety of the top person. There are many occasions when the heat at the top must stop there. One of the more important roles of middle management lies in protecting lower ranks from the uncertainties which produce shudders and trembling in mahogany-paneled offices.

Motivation of workhorses does not mean exhorting them to go faster and do more. Given a work force of people whose contribution lies mainly in applying their competence under the direction of management, application of the basic tenets of MBO is far better than attempting to speed up the work pace or cut corners.

Let your workhorses know what is expected of them in terms of outcomes, and where to go for help and resources when they are needed. Give them freedom to apply their skills and competencies without interference. Don't breathe down their necks if their track record indicates that they are competent, and don't ask a competent worker to explain his or her every move. Show confidence in their competence.

Arrange the information flow so they can tell how well they are doing in their work as they engage in it, thus enlarging the amount of self-control which they wield over their own work station and work processes. Be generous in providing timely recognition and feedback on the success and failure of their efforts.

Enrich their jobs by giving them some kind of client relationship with the people they serve or areas they service.

If we've learned anything at all from the behavioral sciences in the last forty years, it is that all of these things will put such competent people under self-control. People who reward and punish themselves control their own work, and self-control releases their best energies. Deprive people of this support and you thwart that energy.

The Power of Commitment

If employees know what is expected, and what help and resources are available, they can then be relied upon to govern their actions to achieve the commitments they have made. People who make commitments to somebody whose opinion is important to them are practically obliged to do something about those commitments. This is especially true if those commitments have been made in face-to-face discussions, and have been confirmed in writing.

It is the power of commitment that makes MBO work, and the absence of such commitment can cause it to fail.

Under MBO the objectives and constraints are known in advance. People know that they are to achieve their commitments and stay within the constraints, and so can operate freely within these boundaries. This is significantly different from a "Do what you are told to do" rule, which slows down decision making, inhibits innovation, and obstructs excellence at lower levels.

Thomas Peters and Robert Waterman, Jr., in their best-seller, *In*

Search of Excellence, have dramatized for millions of readers the idea of excellence in management at the topmost level. This is highly beneficial, coming at the end of a time when we had become a nation of self-doubters and often self-haters.

Watching stars succeed is a source of great excitement and pleasure for many, whether it's General George Patton leading the Third Army in a sweep across Europe at the end of World War II, Dr. Jonas Salk discovering a vaccine to prevent polio, or Lee Iacocca turning around the ailing Chrysler Corporation. Yet, excellence needs to be expanded to include more than the stars of our organizations.

I am not optimistic enough to believe that everyone who works will be excellent, but we do need excellence and competence at every level of society and at every level of our organizations. We need excellence in balancing our bank statements, preparing budgets, teaching our children, and repairing our automobiles.

Without good grammar-school teachers we cannot retain technical leadership in physics, medicine, and engineering. Without competent maintenance personnel, our machinery will go unserviced, with production grinding to a halt and productivity falling to new lows. Competent ditchdiggers and plumbers can produce sanitary systems which affect good health for more people than the best thoracic surgeon can affect in performing dramatic open-heart operations.

To abandon excellence in any of these areas is to accept mediocrity, goofing off, half-done jobs, and goldbricking. We will decline as a society and, more important, in our own self-esteem. Unless we can manage our workhorses by first imbuing them with a goal of striving for excellence in their work, we can't hope for a steady series of dramatic breakthroughs to carry us onward.

In a world where bright young MBAs ascend to the upper reaches of management by age 35, we may overlook two major requirements in managing our workhorse population.

First, we need to run pluralistic organizations in which honor and respect are built into our personnel policies, our human resources strategies, our pay systems, our benefit plans, and our training courses for workhorses.

Second, we need to recognize the achievement and competence of all of our employees, rather than limit recognition to the few stars who sweep through the organization maze to the top.

You can't build stars in scientific creativity, administration, managerial strategy, and statesmanship in government with a system that wastes the potential of every person at whatever level he or she works. The idea that people who work with their hands are somehow inferior to those who work with ideas at a conference table or at a computer terminal denies self-fulfillment to a majority of our work force.

Personnel programs tied to the basic economics of the portfolio approach to human resources management must be grounded in recognition, belonging, self-esteem, adequacy, and security for everyone who works, however humble his or her position may be. Our management systems need to give everyone a reason and a chance to work at their highest level of competence.

11
Coping with Poor Performance: The Failure of Integration

Human behavior is the most familiar feature of this world in which people live. . . .

—B.F. Skinner

The career of General George Patton illustrates the difficulty of identifying the unsatisfactory performer in an organization. During his cadet years at West Point and early years as an officer in the peacetime army, Patton was often considered a problem child. Rash, impetuous, self-centered, and plainly too outspoken, he was shunted from one post to another as his career floundered. He watched some of his classmates from West Point rise past him, fighting the tea-bouts and white-glove receptions in the army of the thirties. Yet, when the guns began to shoot and they needed a tank commander who could rip through enemy lines and slash the whole order of battle to shreds by his daring and dash, George Patton was called upon. He was a star. Once the war was over, Patton fell back into his old role—a problem child, impolitic, offending his superiors and U.S. allies, drawing unfavorable media attention upon himself and his superiors.

Patton, and perhaps hundreds of others in the military, business, government, the university, and the nonprofit organization, all demonstrate that high performance is in large measure situational. The behavior which is appropriate in one situation isn't in another. The hymns John Smith sings in church aren't the same songs he sings at a bawdy event celebrating the forthcoming marriage of a classmate. The speedy move in one environment may be perfectly suitable, while speed in another produces nothing but disaster.

The situational nature of success and failure on the job is often a failure to integrate the individual and company's needs. It is in understanding this mismatch between job and performer that the idea of management by integration fits in a most helpful way.

Integration doesn't simply mean patching different things together in a seamless whole. When a corporate merger occurs, the acquiring company has a choice whether to operate as a wholly owned subsidiary or to integrate itself into the main company. When the former choice is made, the identity of the new affiliate is retained. In the latter choice it is lost. ITT, for example, owns many firms including the Sheraton Corporation, Hartford Insurance, and the like. While they are clearly the property of ITT, they have separate identities and a considerable amount of autonomy.

In a somewhat similar way, a company can engage workers as independent contractors. They don't join the company, aren't employed by it, don't share the security of employees, and are paid on a project-by-project basis. The contract is the limit of integration. If a contractor were to give up the contractor role and agree to be hired by the company, it would entail certain sacrifices in independence, freedom of choice, and autonomy. It is this integration of employee, retaining an entrepreneurial, independent, and voluntary effort, that the organization hopes to achieve by its supervisory style. When an employee "doesn't work out" or fails to "fit" it may be the fault of the organization, the employee, or the arrangement between them. The worst outcome, from the employee's view, comes when his or her personal identity, values, needs, and individuality are all submerged under organization demands for conformity.

The Problem Employee

There can be a variety of kinds of performance failure in an organization:

1. Former stars, whose performance has slipped and who have now become problem employees.

2. Formerly successful workhorses whose skills have eroded and whose competence has become obsolete.

3. Problem children whose problems have resisted all efforts at correction.

4. Deadwood, for whom no existing or foreseeable remedies show any promise of improvement.

To match these kinds of poor performers, there is a range of possible avenues for solution. The first cluster of solution plans lies in attempts to achieve integration of the person and the organization through changes in the practices of the organization. You might consider, for example, redesigning the job to fit the person, as is done under the law with handicapped employees who require special facilities for access. You might remove some responsibilities from the job which have been causing trouble, and placing them in another place. The receptionist who is an excellent clerical person but has an abrupt or awkward manner of dealing with the public might be moved to a less public position where the secretarial skills that exist will assure success.

Training and development might be shaped to upgrade competencies or teach new ones. Where the organization has an employee assistance program it might solve the problem of absenteeism and tardiness for the single parent by arranging child care or changing work hours. Tardiness might be remedied by transportation pools. Flextime for working parents has become a common response to the problems of employees who must integrate their lives as parents with their lives as employees.

As the number and character of causes of employee problems increase because of the wider variety of people who work, more and more organizations are pursuing organizational changes that help to make integration of the organization and the employee possible. The root of employee assistance programs should be finding organization responses to employee problems. As well as dealing with changing behavior, medical and psychological help, fitness programs, and the many other aspects of "employee benefits" programs are in fact attempts to find organizational responses that will produce integration. It is exactly because of the expansion and diversity of employees and their needs in the nineties that management by integration and self-control has become a paramount issue for management.

Dealing with Individual Incompetence

Despite the best efforts of organizations to create new helping programs, bend their own practices,and create new practices to produce integration, there will undoubtedly be cases where no further measures are practical or economic. In such cases it is the individual who must change or be replaced. John Miner defines four options which can be used for employees who have fallen below the standards of performance or some aspect of performance. They include promotion, transfer, demotion, and disciplinary action, which includes supervisory action to effect a behavior change and reestablish integration.

The problem of the unsatisfactory performer is one that managers cannot afford to neglect. As a famous Supreme Court justice once said, "Every dog deserves one bite." I certainly wouldn't get too uptight about a single error by a subordinate if the person can learn from the mistake. On the other hand I wouldn't suggest that a boss should be as tolerant as the manager of a baseball team in 1903 who allowed a player named Piano Legs Hickman to make a record 91 errors in 118 games. Repeated errors are a signal that an individual is not properly qualified for the job, is in over his or her head, and shouldn't be left in that position to continue fouling things up.

To avoid having a situation get out of hand, set up a control system to watch for poor quality work. Use errors as an occasion for teaching. If the person learns from mistakes, they aren't really all that bad in most cases.

However, if you merely stand around and keep score while the subordinate doesn't improve, you're jeopardizing your own job and you're probably guilty of managerial malfeasance.

When push comes to shove and you need to separate (fire) an unsatisfactory performer, you must first be sure that what you're faced with is really noncorrectable unsatisfactory performance. This means that you must build a case, or, in many situations, your action will be reversed by an arbitrator or a review board.

Due process means letting people know in advance what is expected, giving them sufficient help and freedom to do the job without interference, giving them an interim warning and counseling, and separating them only when all has failed to produce improvement. It's advisable to document every step and to keep good records.

You need to have a book of rules to go by if you are going to fire people for violating rules. You can't invent the rules after the act, nor can the rules be applied unequally among various parts of the organization or among different people.

You can separate people if you meet all of these guidelines, but failure to apply these guidelines could prove embarrassing.

No More Mr. Good-Guy

It's okay to reward your star performers, but it's not okay to "good-guy" your nonperformers. Florence King, in a recent issue of *Harper's,* decries what she perceives as "a constitutional defect in the American Mind." She refers to the "niceness factor," which is also known as "good-guyism." One manifestation of this is that we assign a variety of "nice" names to people rather than calling them what they are: The poor are "culturally disadvantaged" and midgets are "people of reduced stature." It's all part of a national mania for not hurting anyone's feelings, even when such behavior is going to hurt the person more in the long run.

Nowhere is this more apparent than in the inability of business executives and managers in government and other nonprofit organizations to face up to the failure of a subordinate upon whom much responsibility has been laid.

At a recent management conference I polled a group of executives on the question of whether it is now harder or easier to fire somebody than it used to be. About four out of five responded that it's now harder to fire people. This may be because of new laws and the limitations of new government controls, but I would suggest that it's also accounted for in part by the rising tide of "niceness." We let ourselves be patient when all of the evidence (and there's plenty of it, loud and continual) indicates that some action should be taken.

1. When the person knows what is expected but repeatedly fails to perform for some reason or another.

2. When the person knows where to get help and resources but doesn't get them.

3. When the person has been counselled and given time to mend his or her ways but still fails to improve his or her performance.

The action to be taken may be to discharge the employee, but there are other options. Demotion for cause is rare, but it may be tried. Reassignment is more common; it allows you to take a second look at the person's work.

But whatever the remedy, good-guyism should not be the prevailing method of handling problem employees.

It's true that it is necessary to help people save face, but it is neither fair nor decent to hurt the organization, its good performers, and its customers or clients by failing to face up to the problems of employee failure.

Six Steps in Analyzing Poor Performance

Poor performance on the part of individual workers is a test of the manager's basic assumptions about people. Two extreme positions emerge under such pressure.

The punitive manager puts the blame squarely on the offender with the assumption that if a person with high potential doesn't shape up, he or she is deficient in professionalism or has a basic weakness in character. Alternatively, poor performance might be seen as evidence that the person is lacking in brains, skills, or proper attitude, possibly rooted in genetic qualities or in the person's upbringing. Given all of these basic shortcomings, the only sensible course of action is rapid firing, or perhaps other less serious punishment. In effect, this sort of boss brings the wrath of God to bear in such situations.

The developmental manager is diametrically opposed. This type of boss assumes that there is a cause for the poor performance, and before any radical action affecting the employee takes place the boss digs into the situation to find the causes of the poor performance and to correct them. Was it the system which produced the behavior? Was it supervision? Or was it the individual personally? This second approach is developmental and entails a sequence of six steps. The individual may still be disciplined or even discharged, but that's not the first assumption.

Let's look in detail at each of the developmental manager's six steps in analyzing poor performance.

Step 1: Advance Specifications of Performance

Did the individual know in advance that specific performance was expected of him or her? As mentioned earlier, evidence shows that the average manager and subordinate left to their own devices will have different ideas about what is expected of the subordinate. Unless they systematically meet and discuss those expectations in the form of objectives, standards of performance, action required, and criteria for success, it is likely that the subordinate will fail simply for lack of information.

Many employees have been discharged for failing to do something which they didn't know they were responsible for doing. They learn of the expectation after the fact, when the boss, having failed in the basic managerial task of defining objectives for subordinates, focuses upon the failure itself and blames the victim.

The developmental manager makes certain that the subordinate clearly knows in advance what is expected, and what help and resources are available. In addition the developmental manager frees subordinates from undue restrictions or interference, arranges feedback of results while the work is being performed, and defines all expectations clearly in terms of the conditions which will exist if the job is well done or poorly done.

The very fact of finding out what is expected usually improves the performance of subordinates.

Step 2: Removal of Obstacles to Success

Where the punitive manager concentrates on punishing the failure, the developmental manager is supportive. Research into the differ-

ences between successful and unsuccessful managers indicates that
it is a supportive manager who is more likely to produce successful
performance in subordinates.

With clear goals in hand, the subordinate finds that the boss
serves as a helper, supporter, and backup. This involves more than
the provision of ample and suitable tools, equipment, and resources
for the subordinate to get the job done. It often includes the use of
blocking behavior on the part of the boss to eliminate contradictory
signals and actively remove interfering forces which could stop the
subordinate from succeeding.

In specific actions, the supportive boss thinks and acts out the
answers to the question: "Is there anything I could do, do differently, or refrain from doing to help my subordinates succeed?"

Step 3: Access to Training

Many engineers complain that they are thrown into projects and
assignments without consideration of the new and novel requirements of the task in terms of special training, education, and skills
development. Robert Mager suggests that the boss ask the question:
"Could I do this job myself if my life depended upon it?" If the
answer is negative, then training and knowledge acquisition are a
necessary part of the supportive action required of the boss.

Two stories illustrate the problem created by the promotion of
people whose previous experience doesn't correspond with the responsibilities of the new higher-level position:

A firm was plagued by a government contracts division which
consistently lost money. Management responded to the problem by
repeatedly hiring and firing general managers, many of whom had
been very successful in other commercial divisions of the firm. Yet
none had the special knowledge required to direct and develop
strategies for a government contracts operations. Finally, however,
an experienced administrator with government/business experience
was assigned to the job almost by accident, and the division was
turned around.

The John DeLorean story is that of a man who served with distinction and considerable success in the Pontiac, Buick, and Chev-

rolet divisions of General Motors but who was lost, frustrated, and probably out of his element when thrust into a senior corporate-level job at GM. He ultimately resigned. His subsequent career in starting his own firm to produce a sleek new sports car in Northern Ireland and his problems with U.S. narcotics officials are legendary.

Inadequate training in the kinds of knowledge and skills required for a new position is an element in performance failures. Sink-or-swim management will occasionally work when the individual is a fast learner and very adaptive, or when he or she has been self-taught. Failure is likely, however, when the individual is totally untrained.

Step 4: Favorable Consequences

The explanation for many performance failures lies in the kinds of consequences which occur to the individual for behaving right and behaving wrong. If the unfavorable consequences are high for doing the right things, then wrong behavior will ensue and performance failure is predictable.

The president of a small college was made to understand that fund raising was a major part of his responsibility. Yet every time he was absent from the campus, faculty groups complained about their "absentee president." These complaints rose to the trustee level. The board then called him in and politely informed him that he was expected to "run this college" and not be "gallivanting around the country." In view of this, it wasn't surprising that he subsequently failed to produce large sums of money from foundations and philanthropists who were located hundreds of miles from the campus. Since the consequences for doing the right things were unfavorable, he failed, and in the process was charged with being too small for the high rank he held.

Step 5: Feedback on Results

One of the most traumatic shocks which unsuccessful performers can suffer is that of proceeding on a day-to-day basis with the assumption that they are doing well in their work, only to be informed at the end of the period, perhaps a year later, that they have been doing poorly all along. People need to know two kinds of things about their performance:

1. People need to know how well they are doing in their job while actually doing it. This means that a form of continuous feedback is required, not just periodic feedback such as occurs in a year-end performance appraisal or even in a quarterly review.

Self-control by a responsible individual over his or her performance is the most perfect form of control. If the requirements of the job and expectations of the boss have been clearly spelled out—with standards of performance, constraints, and definitions of success and failure set forth in advance—a responsible person is empowered to become a self-rewarder or a self-punisher. Every job should have built-in methods for measuring one's own performance. People should not be obliged to await the verdict of a remote judge after the fact.

This management principle was recognized in Peter Drucker's classic description of MBO in the chapter "Management by Objectives and Self-Control" in his 1954 book, *The Practice of Management*. While the MBO system in many organizations is quite clear in defining outputs sought at the end of the period, it is often less clear in defining standards of performance which the individual may use to operate under self-control. I would suggest that management information systems (MIS) be used for this purpose. At their best, these provide timely, accurate, frequent, and specific knowledge of results to every member of the organization.

2. A summary review of the whole period, including all of the goals and the results attained against them, should be held at the end of the period to revise the goals and set new ones.

This is the point at which performance records are filed. These should include full explanatory statements, not only of the actual goals and results but also any extenuating facts which would explain the behavior.

Step 6: The Personal Factor

If analysis of the five steps above doesn't yield a clue to the cause of the performance failure, attention must logically be turned to the individual. Here the manager faces a whole range of possibilities for the cause of ineffective personal performance, a few of which are noted here:

1. *Physical problems.* A person's health has an important bearing upon his or her performance. As the Age Discrimination in Employment Act lengthens the work-life of employees, it is to be expected that health problems among older employees will increase. This problem, which Mark Lipton called the "unmentionable personnel problem," is rooted in statistical data showing that cancer, heart disease, and other maladies wreak their effects most heavily upon people in their later years. Most large firms now have mandatory annual medical exams for all employees and fitness programs to improve cardiovascular health, not merely to provide a recreational benefit. The sedentary employee, often overweight to the point of obesity, finds that his or her physical condition adversely affects performance, lowers energy, and is a matter of concern for the human resources portfolio manager.

2. *Stress and emotional problems.* Studies of work habits among high-potential people reveal that many of them exhibit Type A behavior, compulsive, nonstop activity that may produce unfavorable emotional and physical health effects. The supervisor of employees with high potential whose performance has declined should recognize Type A behavior and seek professional advice in dealing with stressed subordinates. Stress management courses and groups are now common in many firms. Stress is also often associated with alcohol and other substance abuse. In some states alcoholism is legally considered a disease and medical insurance plans are required to provide treatment for the alcoholic employee.

3. *Personal problems.* Many problem children and even some deadwood in the human resources portfolio are employees who are overwhelmed by off-the-job problems. Employee assistance programs in many firms provide help in dealing with such problems, regardless of their nature.

4. *Work habits.* For some, poor performance is attributable to the ways in which the person goes about doing the job. The results expected from the job may be known, but inefficient approaches and methods of organizing the work may produce failure. Correcting bad work habits is not a project for the firm as a whole; this is

a task which can be adequately handled with coaching and counseling by an employee's immediate supervisor. The employee who disdains the company's procedures, misuses company equipment for personal gain, or fails in a single part of the job due to laxity or faulty work habits probably needs the counseling and direction of a superior.

Ineffective performance should always be investigated by the superior. While the roots of much of this behavior may lie in mental, emotional, or personal causes, it is the responsibility of the supervisor to supervise, to apply progressive discipline, and to confront poor performance, when it occurs, without delay.

Progressive Discipline

"An eye for an eye and a tooth for a tooth"—the Old Testament dictum—typifies the old-fashioned approach to employee discipline. Punishment was designed to fit the crime.

While it is entirely conceivable that a system of retributive justice may originally have had some behavior change objectives, over time such exacting kinds of punishments acquired a character quite apart from the behavior change effect and became an almost divinely inspired system of cause and effect, as if the crime itself produced the specific punishment.

Most discipline, however, must meet a number of new requirements beyond punishment. Concern with human rights and due process of law makes old-fashioned discipline practices obsolete. Even in cases where no labor union exists, the grievance procedures and the right to appeal are increasingly being used in disciplinary cases.

The modern behavioral approach to discipline is composed of two major segments: (1) A list of actions, regulations, rules, behaviors, or offenses which shall trigger the corrective and remedial process; and (2) a set of procedures which shall be put into action when such offenses occur.

In all human organizations there are kinds of behavior that cannot be permitted, for they keep the organization from going toward its objectives, prevent individual members from doing their own work, or interfere with the personal rights of others. Such offenses are traditionally listed in order of seriousness and according to the severity of the ultimate punishments which might be used in the corrective process. These may be noted as falling into categories of major, moderate and minor offenses.

Discipline in the workplace has six special features that are not characteristic of discipline elsewhere. These differences center around the objectives and the purposes of the organization.

1. Discipline at work is for the most part voluntarily accepted. If it is not voluntarily accepted, it is not legitimate.

2. Discipline is a shaper of behavior, not a punishment system. Disciplinary action should serve to provide favorable consequences for the right behavior and unfavorable consequences for improper behavior.

3. The past provides useful experience in defining and changing behavior, but it is not an infallible guide to right and wrong. The boss who suggests "Do it my way the first time, then, after thinking about it, introduce improvements if you can" senses the importance of using experience while encouraging innovation.

4. Contribution to objectives is a reasonable guide as to when to depart from rules and regulations. Slavishly adhering to rules and regulations that carry a person away from his or her objectives is as bad as violating rules that carry one toward the objectives. Refusing to worship laws and rules as having a special mystique of their own is excellent; refusing to hate them blindly is equally sound. One who breaks rules does so at his or her own risk.

5. All rules and regulations should be reviewed periodically against the objectives of the organization to see if they are still productive.

6. The exceptional performer who is achieving exceptional results should be treated with far greater tolerance when it comes to violation of rules and regulations. This implies a converse rule. The cavalier treatment of ordinary rules of conduct is permissible only to people of exceptional competence and achievement. People whose performance is routine should adhere to the rules until such time as they display an ability to produce at an exceptional level.

Make Discipline a Teaching Process

The distinction being made here is between antisocial acts such as robbery and other crimes of violence (which are subject to the same kinds of discipline whether they occur on the job or in the street) and the finely honed requirements of conformity to the will of the boss on the job (which need to be handled so as to change non-productive behavior into productive behavior).

To make the disciplinary process a teaching and behavior-change action, seven conditions must be met:

1. Rules and regulations must be devised and made known.
2. Corrective action should be taken as close to the time of a violation as is feasible. Holding off discussions of personal behavior lapses until the annual performance review lessens the behavior-change effect.
3. The accused person should be presented with facts and with the source of those facts.
4. If a specific rule has been broken, you should state that rule.
5. The reason for the rule should also be stated.
6. Turn the conversation toward objectives and away from excuses or alibis. Ask the apparent offender if he or she agrees with the facts as you have stated them; then ask what his or her objectives were in following the behavior pursued. Asking for one's objectives opens the door for discussion about choosing a behavior pattern that is more productive and can lead to future improvement.
7. State corrective action in positive and forward-looking terms, emphasizing contribution to objectives.

All of this assumes, of course, that your rules and regulations are in fact consistent with your objectives. The development of sound disciplinary policy requires that the personnel department initiate and maintain a regular review of rules of conduct for the plant or office. Such a review should deal with rules as they presently exist and with what contribution the rules make toward objectives. Some typical contributions to objectives of work rules include:

Prevents spoilage and repair costs.

Prevents line shutdown.

Prevents customer complaints about quality.

Ensures safety of fellow workers.

Ensures safety of the employee.

Improves yield of production line.

Prevents tool breakage.

Prevents overexpenditure for small tools.

For some rules that seem to have vast powers of survival, only the following responses can be found:

We've always done it that way.

It's our policy.

That rule was made after many long years of experience.

Our last boss (now retired) installed that one.

Because I want it, dammit.

I don't have the time to explain it to you; just do it.

It's generally a good thing.

You wouldn't really understand why, so let's not discuss it.

Don't make waves.

If these are the justifications, the rule should be eliminated unless further study reveals some valid contribution that it makes to the objectives of the organization.

The Four Stages of Disciplinary Action

The application of discipline should be progressive, though for certain kinds of offenses—murder, rape, felonious assault, major theft, deliberate damage to company property—the first offense is the last, since it is cause for immediate discharge.

Lesser offenses should be subject to the application of disciplinary actions in stages, each stage moving closer to separation but each one in turn designed to effect a behavior change prior to that move. These stages generally include:

Stage I: First Offense

Instruct the employee in the proper method, explain the rule and its reasons, and explain what the next level of discipline will be for a repeat offense. Report the incident in the employee's personnel record.

Stage II: Second Offense

If it is a repeat of the first offense, summarize the instructions, tell the individual that this is a second offense, issue a reprimand, and inform the employee that a third offense will be met with a temporary layoff without pay. Explain the reasons for the rule. Report the incident in the employee's personnel record. If the second offense is of a similar magnitude to the first but different in specifics, instruct the employee in the proper method, warn of the next step that follows a third offense, and report the incident in the employee's personnel record.

Stage III: Third Offense

The supervisor should at this stage consult with his or her superior and with the personnel department, since the issue might become arbitrational. Having verified that a Stage III offense has occurred, instruct the individual and issue a layoff of two to five days without pay, along with a warning that a repeat of any similar level offense will result in discharge and the marking of the person's record to prevent reemployment with the organization. Report the incident in the employee's personnel record.

Stage IV: Discharge

Following a confirmation from the supervisor's superior and the personnel department, the supervisor should tell the offender that he or she is discharged. This should be reported in the employee's personnel record along with a recommendation on rehiring or not rehiring.

This brief description of the four stages of disciplinary action is based upon the successful experience of managers in unionized organizations and of government supervisors who have discharged employees and have been upheld in doing so.

Throughout the entire process it should be borne in mind that each move made by the superior may subsequently be subjected to close scrutiny by an arbitrator, a review board, a top executive of the organization, or maybe even a judge.

Nine Rules for Supervisors

In addition to knowing the four general stages of disciplinary action, the supervisor should adhere to certain rules that govern the entire disciplinary process. Failure to observe these nine rules could result in the reversal of any disciplinary action taken.

1. Be certain that the rule exists, that it is clear, and that the employees know it.

2. Use a statute of limitations rule of six to twelve months for minor incidents, two to three years for layoff reports.

3. Avoid verbal and physical behavior on your part that might create further incidents.

4. Be consistent in applying the four stages of discipline to different people.

5. Listen carefully to what the other person says at all times and note the substance of his or her remarks in the personnel record.

6. Be certain of your facts before making your decision.

7. Don't allow emotional pressures to cause you to jump over disciplinary stages for less than discharge offenses. This is the most likely cause of reversal by an arbitrator, who will reduce the penalty to what it should have been.

8. When a laid-off employee returns to work, treat him or her like any other employee. Don't continue the punishment.

9. Avoid entrapment; that is, don't encourage or entice employees to break rules for the purpose of catching and then disciplining them.

How to Respond to Nonrule Offenses

Not all offensive behavior is a violation of rules. Certain kinds of behavior that do not fall clearly under the rules still require supervisory attention and correction.

An example is the salesman who loses sales by telling offensive jokes. He should be made to see how his behavior damages his performance. Telling jokes is not in itself bad, and identifying what type of joke is offensive can be difficult, because what one person likes another might dislike. But clearly if the behavior causes sales to be lost, it needs to be changed.

The boss shouldn't lecture on what is offensive, berate the salesman for stupidity, use satire or sarcasm, sympathize or agree, or tell the salesman what to do. The emphasis in responding to nonrule offenses should be upon behavior change, through concentrating on what would constitute responsible behavior in the future.

Once the employee recognizes the objective and the problem, he or she can start discussing some optional plans for solving the problem. What appears to be a disciplinary matter becomes a teaching and coaching incident.

There is no useful purpose in writing up such an incident in the employee's personnel record. The people-centered manager who builds competent subordinates through coaching has hundreds of such incidents each year. They comprise the ordinary fabric of management and should not be treated as disciplinary incidents.

This blending of discipline and coaching, or remedial rather than punitive discipline, is centered around the achievement of objectives rather than the extermination of sin.

Don't Create Vengeful Employees

A favorable word from the boss can make us feel good. It increases self-esteem, our liking for ourselves. Even when we suspect that the boss is merely showing good manners, or following some stylistic form, we still cling to the kind words because our self-esteem needs such nourishment. From the time the doctor first lifts us off the natal table and whacks us on the behind to produce a healthy yell, our self-esteem gets slapped around by life. So anybody important who makes a moderate effort to build our self-esteem is bound to be deeply appreciated.

On the other side of the coin, there are times when a boss simply can't lavish praise upon people, because they've goofed up and need to be told about it so that they won't do so again. After all, teaching and coaching are important responsibilities of a boss. But there is a trap that must be avoided in the process of admonishing and coaching the unsatisfactory performer. It's possible that the way in which you correct unsatisfactory performance may turn the problem employee into a dangerously hostile one. This is what I call the "dark side of motivation." Instead of solving the problem of unsatisfactory performance, you create a whole host of new problems that may be difficult—if not impossible—to solve.

In the process of correcting a subordinate the boss may destroy motivation, turning an employee into a vengeful person whose major goal in life is getting even, in order to restore his or her self-esteem.

Greg Rochlin, the Harvard psychologist who has studied the question of self-esteem in depth, proposes, in effect, that people have storage tanks of self-esteem, and that when a person's supply of self-esteem is drained or drops below some safety level, that person's behavior becomes aggressive.

In the process of discipline and coaching, bosses need to recognize the limits to which they can stretch people. Tell me that I have failed once or twice and I can live with that, but tell me that I'm a failure and my self-esteem is endangered. I may be unable to adapt, and may seek revenge for the damage done to my self-esteem. I would be most likely to become aggressive and vengeful if I felt in any way that the boss had invented the standards after the game was over so that I couldn't win.

Studies of many kinds of problem managers, professionals, and employees show that they are apt to be disaffected, carrying around enormous loads of vengeance—a sort of negative motivation—toward the organization, the boss, or some individual manager.

Consultant Jack Bologna has studied computer rip-offs and finds that three conditions exist in a majority of the big thefts. First, the thief has computer skills. Second, the person has access to the computer system. Third, the person is disaffected and has strong vengeful feelings toward the organization.

Bosses who callously destroy the self-esteem of an employee in a fit of displeasure at some action or failure to act often unleash forces which will boil and fume inside the organization, leading to endless mischief and damage. The famous mad bomber of New York many years ago proved to be a disaffected employee of a public utility who felt he had been robbed of a deserved raise. Terrorists, saboteurs, and people who simply engage in malicious obedience are most likely to be working out their revenge against an early boss or employer, a cruel parent, or some other kind of repressor who has robbed them of their self-esteem.

Revenge is pervasive in our society. Getting even is an understandable motive that seems to transform any sort of behavior, even the most antisocial, into something quite explainable and even noble.

The basic plot of every western movie ever made is vengeance. Even Jesse James was avenging a wrong done to his mother and sister.

People join unions to seek revenge for slights and rejections which blew the self-esteem of workers out of the water sometime in the distant past (although this certainly isn't the only explanation for unionism).

Recent events in Northern Ireland, in Lebanon and Israel, in India and Pakistan, and even in Japanese-American trade relations have traces of revenge in them.

Young people sometimes pursue a career with extraordinary vigor to show up some long-dead elder who slighted them or who downgraded their potential and ability in a casually cast slur.

The person who is fired—even justly—may spend an inordinate amount of time in sticking knives into the former employer.

Our language reveals how we feel about revenge. Getting even, we say, means "putting things right." And when revenge comes, it's generally described as being "sweet." We even attach Old Testament religious values to vengeance ("an eye for an eye"). The hours, days, months, or even years of work and effort spent in seeking revenge are considered a small price to pay for the sweet moment when "justice" is done.

There are, however, some instances in which the desire for revenge is turned into constructive channels. Last year's defeat, for instance, can become the motive for the extra work and energy needed to win this year. But turning an ordinary, lackadaisical subordinate into a vengeful person is hardly worth the price.

The Damage of Revenge Seeking

It's an often-overlooked fact that the major damage done in vengeance seeking is done to the vengeful individual, not to his or her target. Vengeance seeking usually changes the intentions and goals of the avenger, transforming the individual.

Many psychiatrists have said that it is difficult—some say impossible—to change the personality of a person by ordinary therapeutic methods. Yet, when you become a vengeance seeker, exactly that effect can occur. No amount of pain, difficulty, or elapsed time will dim the desire to get even when the hurt to your self-esteem is sharp enough or great enough.

The antidote to falling into such a fruitless and damaging mood lies in mind over emotion (or self-mastery—taking command of your own life, rather than allowing yourself to be mastered by your enemies). The solution is also suggested by the religious precept of turning the other cheek, which is sound mental health advice.

The size of a person is often measured by the size of his or her enemies, and by the size of the issues about which they become angry or vengeful. Don't let yourself get turned onto a vengeful course by small affronts to your self-esteem.

Some people spend their lives going about looking for affronts that they can turn into reasons for vengeance. They don't manage their lives; they are managed by even the least important people around them who inflict real or imagined insults upon them.

Being able to manage your own life is probably a necessary first step to being a manager. If you are going to be entrusted to manage General Electric, the Bell System, a 500-bed hospital, or a regional Social Security Administration office, it's probably a sound idea to get your own affairs under management first. Toleration of small blows to your self-esteem, psychological paper cuts, or bumps and bruises picked up in scrimmage is the first step to self-management.

If you find yourself thirsting for vengeance and acting on the adage "Don't get mad, get even," back off and start thinking more broadly about your own self-interest. You really cannot afford vengeance motives and feuds that divert you from getting on with the main business at hand.

Even when vengeance is impossible, it works its dark results on the individual. Maybe the person you want to get even with has disappeared, died, or moved away. In such cases the vengeance motive is likely to turn inward.

Eric Berne described this as a game people play called "Now look what you made me do." One example is that of the spouse who can't get even who turns to such things as nagging, philandering, or having four martinis on the way home from the office each night.

Employees who can't fight back may dive into a pitched battle, or become addicts of other habits which ultimately destroy them. Self-hatred, expressed as a fear of success, can be turned into a self-righteous justification of failure. ("I could have been an executive but I was stopped by that bastard Jones.")

The kid who threatens to hold his breath until he dies because his mother denies him something has many counterparts among adult vengeance seekers who insist upon punishment, even if it's only they themselves who get punished. Such a perverse reaction is more likely to occur when the force which robbed the person of his or her self-esteem isn't an individual but an organization or a system which is hard to fight. When revenge is demanded and you can't fight city hall or corporate policy, you punish yourself by persistently clinging to your vengeance motive.

Don't Attack Employee Self-esteem

What can a hard-pressed boss do when confronted with inferior performance? Should a boss avoid dressing down his or her subordinates and bringing them up short for their failures? Not at all. But there are right and wrong ways of dealing with unsatisfactory performance. The cardinal rule is to stick to specifics of the failure, skipping the sort of sweeping generalizations that would attack the other person's self-worth and self-esteem.

What you can do is say: "Here is what you said you would do, and here is what you actually did. Since the latter doesn't equal the former as it should, I think that you should explain the reasons for the difference to me."

Psychologist Carl Rogers, in discussing sensitivity training, warns trainers never to attack another's defenses but to stick with a discussion of specific behavior. This is acceptable to the other person. For example, telling a person that "I felt disappointed because I wasted an hour waiting for you when you failed to keep your appointment" is substantially different from telling the person that "You are a rotten procrastinator."

It's necessary to tell people that they've failed when they've failed, but it's not necessary or even useful to call them a failure. The former is a matter of fact; the latter is a conclusion which attacks the individual's basic personality structure.

This personality structure is something that is built up to help people cope, and when you pound away at a person's coping mechanism you may break it, causing them to feel the need to seek vengeance.

When you come home from work and see that the lawn still has not been mowed when your son said he'd mow it that afternoon, you should say: "I see that you didn't mow the lawn this afternoon as you said you would," not "You're an unreliable little loafer and good-for-nothing."

If your secretary comes in to work some morning dressed in clothes that you consider unsuitable for the office, tell her not to wear those clothes to work again, not that she looks like a hippie or a cocktail waitress.

The basic rule in coaching people to improve poor performance is to stick with specifics of behavior and results. The name of the game is behavior, not personality. Bear in mind that "behavior" is activity you can see or measure; "personality" means the coping strategies that are defenses against life and its knocks. An attack upon an individual's personality creates an enemy who will somehow find vengeance—on you, on the organization, or upon himself or herself.

In addition to criticizing very specific behavior, the boss should also be ready to give some suggestions for what the person should do, do differently, or stop doing in order to improve his or her performance.

My final comment, which may seem self-evident to you, is that it's also important that the boss not use the occasion of coaching and disciplinary action to get revenge upon people for their errors. The revenge motive is not something that engages only subordinates. Many an irritated boss has decided to wreak vengeance upon an offender and, in the process, starts the fatal cycle of counter-vengeance. Unless we as humans can learn to break this vengeance and countervengeance cycle in our own lives, the world will one day be turned into a rubble of atomic ashes.

Good performance behavior is what we pay for and it's what we have a full right to expect. Beyond that, it's best to allow people to keep their self-esteem as you coach and counsel them on their behavior and results.

12
Productivity: The Integration of Economics and People

Productivity is a much discussed economic term, but it also has a powerful human dimension.

—John Merwin

Thirty miles north of Columbus, in Marysville, Ohio, is the Honda of America plant. There in a modern, landscaped, and highly automated plant, 2,200 workers produce 875 cars a day. About 100 miles north of this plant, in Toledo, the AMC Jeep plant produces 750 cars a day, employing 5,400 workers to do the job. At Honda, a new employee starts at $10.60 an hour. The rates at the AMC Jeep plant are in line with UAW union rates and run almost twice that figure. Admittedly the Honda plant, being only a few years old, is engineered better with more robots, more automation, and better layout. But the explanation for the productivity difference lies almost as much in the attitudes and performance of the work forces.

On the day last fall that the hunting season started, over 15 percent of the Jeep work force stayed away and the other 85 percent were sent home—the plant was shut down completely because of absenteeism. Honda the same day had an absenteeism of 2 percent, which is about average for Honda. Obviously something is different—radically different—between the two plants. It adds up to productivity as a joint result of management practices, including strategy and operational methods, and the integration of workers into the workplace.

Productivity is a relationship between inputs and outputs. When you put a business or organization together, you "put in" resources, capital, equipment, plant, materials and supplies, and labor. You then engage in the process of production, and what comes out (output) should be greater than the sum of the inputs. The difference is value added, called profit in a corporation or business. In a government agency, the output may be program results, patients served, clients processed, lives saved, kids educated, and so on.

While the story of Honda and Jeep is a horror story of comparative productivity, the major problem for the future probably won't lie in American factories. The United States has been fighting back, and in some companies, such as Chrysler, management and the workers have shown that they can bite the bullet and work together to reach higher levels of productivity at lower cost. The common element—productivity—is the unifying goal which can be used as the basis for measuring how well integration and self-control works in practice. Yet most jobs in the United States in the future won't be in manufacturing but in service. Those are the white-collar jobs, the knowledge worker positions.

American Productivity

One of the more fashionable fads these days is to deplore the declining level of productivity in the United States. While a lot of wailing goes on, the situation isn't really all that bad if you consider a few hard facts about what happened between 1970 and 1980:

The U.S. gross national product (GNP) went from $1,085 to $1,502 trillion in 1972 dollars.

Domestic production rose from $563 billion to $1,417 trillion in inflated dollars.

Twenty million new jobs were added.

The productivity index increased from 107 to 147, using 1967 as 100.

Investment as a percentage of GNP rose from 10.5 to 10.7 percent.

The industrial production index rose from 108 to 152.

While these statistics show some softening in the rate of increase, there were declines in only two areas—the take-home pay of workers and the growth rate in real GNP. But the growth rates in real GNP also declined in Japan (from 10.5 to 5.9 percent), in Europe (from 4.7 to 3.5 percent), and in Russia (from 5.0 to 0.6 percent).

One of the favorite games of the self-doubters is to use percentages rather than hard numbers to make their point (which was, I suspect, determined before they ever started digging for facts to support it). The actual numbers tell a different story. It's certainly impressive that corporate profits grew from $71 billion in 1970 to $182 billion in 1980. But this doesn't mean that management should rest on its haunches and assume that nothing needs to be done about productivity. Unless we keep moving onward, we'll be in some trouble by 1990.

Where to Focus Your Major Efforts

Many years ago I was a time-study man in a factory in New Jersey. After about a week of training I was armed with a clipboard and a stopwatch and was sent forth from job to job timing the hapless help. I was supposed to come up with ratings for each job, telling people how much they should produce. All of this had a pretty logical air to it. First I would list on the chart in sequence all of the various elements of the job. Then I would pick a typical or normal performer—who the hell that ever was—and would time that person again and again, not just for completing the whole cycle but for every tiny element of the cycle. Having done this a couple of dozen times, I would then apply some preset formulas and construct an "ideal time" that would become the standard for that job. A bonus was paid to workers who exceeded the standard; otherwise one merely got paid the base hourly rate.

Bemused at my own scientific tools and the special status it gave me among the workers, I bustled importantly into a department one Monday and fastened upon a job that required a worker to pick up square sheets of metal and insert them into a press, where they would be formed into ends for pails. The job was being done by

Angelo, a man old enough to be my father, who had been doing that job for more time than I had been alive. He smiled constantly and was, as I noted on my form, "cooperative."

As I recall the job, it had about eleven steps. I timed each one to a hundredth of a second, and did it again and again. Then I averaged the whole shebang about five different ways according to the formulas I had been taught in the classroom. When I completed my calculations, it was very clear and scientifically unassailable that the standard time for doing this job once was .4591 minutes. Thus, I figured that Angelo could produce two pail-ends every minute, 120 an hour, or 9,600 per day, less an allowance for personal fatigue and delay time. The company could now price the labor cost exactly, and hence the product.

Angelo had kept smiling as I worked seriously at timing his efforts. Still smiling benignly when I was done, he asked: "How did you make out, kid? I would guess that you came out about forty-five or forty-six hundredths of a minute for the cycle. Am I right?"

I was astonished. How could this unlettered old man without the benefit of a stopwatch, clipboard, and training course have arrived at the figure which had taken me a couple of sweaty-palmed hours to engineer? My jaw dropping, I asked him how he did it.

"Hell, kid," he said, "I been timed dozens of times and I know how you do that rubbish. Do ya wanna see some different rates? Watch this, here's a ninety-hundredths of a minute cycle."

With no apparent slowdown he began slipping metal sheets into the press at a different pace. I was stung to the quick and ran a few fast calculations on his new pace. It came out shy of a minute by a tenth, just as he said.

"Now watch this if you wanna see a cycle that runs a quarter of a minute." He said as he once again changed his style and began shooting metal into the press like a smooth machine, becoming a part of the mechanism.

I took a couple of timings and, sure enough, this guy could average anywhere from fifteen seconds to fifty-five seconds per cycle, and I was damned if I could tell the difference by watching him work. My timings were all expert and flawless, according to the system I had learned in class. The daily output on this job could range anywhere between 4,500 and 19,000 pail-ends a day, and just which level of output would actually be achieved was under Angelo's control, not mine, and not the company's.

I retreated to the nearest men's room for a cigarette and to think about this whole experience. There I arrived at a momentous conclusion:

The level of productivity of a worker is very possibly under the control of the worker and not some natural law.

I learned that all of my industrial engineering techniques couldn't really tell whether or not we were getting everything we wanted. Only the worker could control the pace of output.

I learned this lesson in a factory in New Jersey in 1939, but it's a lesson that is learned over and over every year by managers, even those in the supersystematized, automated, integrated, computerized, strategized, and MBO-centered companies of the eighties.

If you automate the job and make it machine-paced, you settle for a mean which people have to keep up with. This means that before the day begins you throw away any extra contribution that workers might make if they made up their own minds to increase their productivity that day.

On the other hand, if the job is not machine-paced (as in a service job, for instance), then you are clearly at the mercy of the worker for making day-by-day and minute-by-minute choices about what level of productivity he or she will put out for the good old company.

Since most workers these days work in service jobs rather than on assembly lines, it seems that we are clearly moving more and more toward a world in which workers can decide for themselves— and, incidentally, the company—what productivity should be and what it will be. No amount of screaming, order-giving, and hell-raising by people in three-piece suits with degrees in finance from Harvard or Stanford apparently can do a thing about it.

The most constructive action for improving productivity is for managers to figure out why people behave the way they do and then to shape their management systems into patterns which will result in people wanting to produce more.

The major inputs in service organizations are knowledge and skills. As Alvin Toffler suggests in his book *The Third Wave,* a whole new kind of society is emerging that's based upon the application of human intelligence. But management isn't moving as fast as society in adapting to change. We're still trying to strap employees into the molds of the industrial society. To overcome this, I suggest following a three-part behavior change cycle:

1. We can aim more directly at enlarging the knowledge and skills of people at work by making stronger commitments to education and training. "Money tree companies," as I call them, already do this.

2. We can study and control the institutional variables which produce the environment at work. People like Angelo respond more to the environment than to rules and orders. The physical environment in which people work, the information they get about their jobs and what's expected of them, and what opportunities and incentives exist for them are all important ingredients of the environmental situation. We need to learn more about group processes and how to apply that knowledge on the job. In addition, we need to identify the obstacles that confront workers in service jobs and keep these intelligent and highly educated people from being more productive.

3. Finally, we must personalize work more by improving the face-to-face transactions that produce commitments to objectives from responsible people.

Writing Objectives to Improve Productivity

When it comes to writing objectives to increase productivity, managers should concentrate on improving the relationship between inputs and outputs. You not only set targets for budgets, you also insist on some corresponding goals for the results of those expenditures.

Setting objectives that focus upon productivity often means devising new ratios, and setting up the improvement of those ratios as indicators of results. For example, a ratio of direct to indirect costs might be established as one indicator of results.

In the early days of setting objectives at General Electric, a team of managers formed the "measurements committee" to study and select the indicators that would best reflect the firm's true goals.

Accountants are experts in numbers, but it's the line managers who must decide what indicators should be set, measured, and reported back.

As Frank Cary, the former president of IBM, told his people: "Add value, not costs." Adding value is the key to improving productivity, in service organizations as well as in manufacturing firms.

Managing High-Talent Workers

Two hundred years ago when the early industrialists broke the cycle of cottage industry and brought workers to factories, great gains were made in productivity. They made the division of labor possible and perfected it. Yet in the process they generated a kind of soulless and depersonalized environment that produced resistance, apathy, anger, and alienation for many workers.

A reversal of this impersonal style of management is needed today to get the high-talent specialist to be more productive and creative.

You can maximize the output of physical labor through the proper division of labor, by mechanizing and automating jobs, and by paying people well for their time. But these things don't work for creating an environment to encourage the knowledge worker.

Geary Rummler, a prominent behavior change consultant, suggests that there are five variables in the performance system that must be managed in order to improve productivity among knowledge workers:

1. The job situation—or the occasion to perform—demands serious attention.

2. The well-educated performer has different goals and expectations than other workers.

3. A clearer definition of actions and decisions needed is required for every job and jobholder.

4. Careful diagnosis of the consequences upon the new high-talent employee of good or bad performance must be sharply defined.

5. Feedback and performance review are needed to provide specific knowledge of results as measured against job objectives.

Productivity in the eighties must be focused on changing work environments to produce conditions in which high-talent people can find satisfaction and benefits. Without that focus, every other orthodox means of increasing productivity will be fruitless.

Misdirected Management Efforts

The U.S. Department of Commerce estimates that the service sector now accounts for as much as 65 percent of the gross national product and for seven of every ten jobs. The growth of service industries is mind-boggling, and not unsurprisingly seems to have left American management with a misconception of what kind of business it is really in. It's not just the economic dimensions of this shift that are important, but the effects that this shift have on managerial practices.

Many of today's senior executives were schooled in product-centered companies where the emphasis was upon manufacturing and marketing. But they are apt to be working in service industry firms today, which calls for some different kinds of employees and different kinds of managerial leadership. The fact that we aren't doing as well as we might in world competition with nations such as Japan may well be rooted in the cultural lag of our top managers. You simply don't run a bank, insurance company, accounting firm, advertising agency, hotel, wholesale and retail firm, transportation business, engineering company, architectural and construction firm, information business, or educational enterprise the same way you do an automobile factory, flour mill, appliance company, or meat-packing plant. There is a growing gap between the practices of management and the needs of the customers, the employees, and the managers.

Daniel Bell, the Harvard sociologist, called the tune on this change very clearly back in the fifties when he predicted that we were on the verge of what he called the "postindustrial society." More recently, Alvin Toffler described the same thing in *The Third Wave.*

The most important products in the postindustrial society, Bell predicted, wouldn't be hardware and products, but knowledge, information, and services. The most important social institutions, he suggested, would be the think tank, the laboratory, the university, and the government agency, as well as the giant corporations which produce software and services.

The growth of the service industry is apparent not only at home but also in the international marketplace. While we've been taking a pasting in world markets in automobiles, appliances, and textiles, our success in selling services abroad has grown by leaps and bounds. The U.S. balance of payments had a surplus in 1985 for the first time in many years, due almost totally to the growth in services sold abroad. Transportation and communications brought in some $14 billion, while banking and financial services generated $24 billion. Construction, oil and gas field services, tanker operations, and engineering services all were multibillion-dollar businesses in our export trade.

At home we see the most rapid growth in computers and information systems, health care, educational services (including publishing), technical services, travel, hotels, food services, and leisure activities (including cable television and electronic games).

While we all agree on the figures, we often fail to see the full implications that this radical shift in our industrial society has for the management of people who work in the service sector. For one thing, our concern—some might even say obsession—with productivity is centered almost exclusively upon increasing the output of autoworkers, steelworkers, factory employees, and the like, who in fact make up the smallest part of our business establishment.

Quality circles, for example, have been limited mostly to hourly rated workers on the plant floor to increase their productivity and morale. Few if any of the reported applications have occurred in advertising agencies, construction engineering firms, or research and development labs. Yet it is exactly in service areas like these where most workers are employed.

Opinion Research Corporation recently surveyed the entire spectrum of workers at all levels, including supervisory and middle management, and found that morale and confidence are at the lowest levels ever recorded. In effect, current management practices have been geared to a kind of worker and to a form of organization which is no longer all that significant today. They have overlooked the needs of the majority of workers and managers.

Service Organizations Can't Use Autocratic Leadership

People have become educated at higher levels than ever before, in the United States and Canada and around the world. In the process of being educated, they have acquired certain new expectations regarding their lives and their work which, if denied, produce frustration, anger, and apathy.

For one thing, workers now expect to participate in the decisions that affect them. Yet they work in a world where orders, for the most part, come from the top and in which there is less opportunity to talk back and to be listened to than they see as desirable and necessary. Under pressure to produce short-term profits for investors and the people who determine stock prices, managers reward people who demonstrate that they can get immediate results. While all of this may be fine and good in many ways, it also leads to management styles that are often unnecessarily hard-nosed, autocratic, domineering, and indifferent to the needs of the people who make things happen, who staff the key positions, and who direct the major units which produce the services being sold.

For instance, many service firms, particularly in the advertising and brokerage industries, believe in firing people upon the first offense, or even upon no offense, as an ordinary, daily tool of control, rather than as a last resort.

All of this flows back into business schools where the young managers are trained. It would be hard to overestimate the importance of the training that MBAs receive in finance and computer-based business skills. But far too many of these people come forth into the business world without understanding the vital role played by managerial styles that keep the troops satisfied and fulfilled in their work. To blame the business schools alone for this would not be fair, however; they simply reflect what the market asks for and pays for.

For far too many seasoned senior executives and rising young managerial superstars, the whole idea of participative management is a snow job, a kind of sentimental rubbish. Only a very few of them realize that participative management, when skillfully and professionally applied, is a strong contributor to getting the profit-making job done, not an impediment.

When *Fortune* magazine last year published a list of the ten toughest managers, few of them were insulted and, to my knowledge, none thought of suing the publisher for defamation of character. Most of them became objects of admiration and emulation. What many managers have overlooked is how many of those same tough guys have subsequently been fired themselves, or how poor the future prospects of their firms appear because there are no competent replacements waiting in the wings to take over should the tough guy die or be fired.

Banks, insurance companies, and hotels, along with other service firms, live—and die—by the skill of their professionals and technical experts. The wit, wisdom, experience, knowledge, and brainpower of their managers and employees are what distinguish the successful firms from the unsuccessful; this is what makes them competitive, or noncompetitive.

Only a few service businesses, however, spend any money training their managers in the human relations aspects of the business. The majority rely upon military-style leadership which not only doesn't work in service businesses but also no longer works in the military (as General David Jones, chairman of the Joint Chiefs of Staff, has been telling the military establishment for many years).

This doesn't mean, of course, that *all* of the behavioral science material we're exposed to is perfectly suitable and useful, but there are some basic ideas which need to be implanted in the managerial practices in service firms if they are to succeed in the nineties. These are the systems that have been tried successfully in some of the leading service organizations, and which the less successful haven't tried.

Merrill Lynch, the giant financial services firm, formerly a brokerage house, is clearly among the leaders in blending humanistic and economic styles of management. Merrill Lynch has shown an uncommon interest in building competent people through extensive training in all aspects of management. It isn't surprising that they, more than any other firm in the industry, operate under a sophisticated and extensive MBO system. Their managers attend an executive academy to learn all of the nuances of modern management in the postindustrial society.

Similarly, Citibank stands out in its field as a company which avoids the kinds of outmoded managerial practices which characterize the typical bank.

IBM retains its leadership in computers not only by being technically and financially strong but also by providing training for every person holding managerial responsibility. It is said that they spent more than a billion dollars on training in 1985, not only for employees but also for customers.

My own research indicates that there are clear differences in the way that people are managed and in how they respond to that management which separate successful service firms from those that fall behind. Here, then, are ten keys to managing the new service-centered business and its people:

1. Clearly define everyone's responsibilities in no uncertain terms. Make sure that everyone knows in advance just what is expected of him or her each year.

2. Establish standards of performance for each area of responsibility.

3. Make sure that all decisions for establishing those responsibilities and standards of performance involve a face-to-face discussion between the boss and the subordinate. You cannot run an organization by sprinkling the place with memoranda and letters.

4. Listen to people before you fix responsibility and seek commitments. This is essential for getting commitment.

5. Use self-control as the major system for keeping the organization on track. If people are clear on their responsibilities and have a reason for doing the job, self-control is the tightest and best form of control.

6. Give people plenty of feedback on how well they are doing in their work, preferably by having a system that lets them

know their results while they are doing their jobs, not necessarily by personal criticism. The self-rewarder and self-punisher is the best employee.

7. Demonstrate clearly that you care about the person's success . . . and failure.

8. Show enthusiasm and support for the efforts of your subordinates, indicating that you are there more to help than to judge.

9. Tie your rewards to performance, and make pay and responsibility, along with rank, a function of an employees's contribution.

10. Work very hard at encouraging people to grow in competence, skills, and status.

If each of these ten points seems quite commonplace to us, maybe we should ask why it is then that they are so commonly overlooked by so many of today's managers, especially by those in service-centered organizations.

Improving White-Collar Productivity

The handwriting is on the wall. Major banks—especially those with troubled loans—are slashing away at expenses, and just about everyone they employ is a white-collar worker. In the hospital industry, severe pressures are being felt from profit-making hospital corporations that apply conventional business management methods to hospital administration. In addition, the health care market is becoming competitive. Insurance companies, manufacturing firms, and service industry businesses all report that they are taking a hard look at their white-collar ranks to find ways of cutting excessive costs.

The productivity of white-collar workers hasn't risen in proportion to the increase in their numbers. While most firms don't have a comprehensive plan for reducing white-collar costs (which presently run around $40,000 per person per year), you can bet that they will be thinking about this more seriously through the rest of the decade. There are a number of different steps or approaches that organizations can take to improve white-collar productivity.

1. The Meat-ax Approach

A program of across-the-board cuts is perhaps the most common and most unfortunate response to reducing overhead costs of white-collar labor. Hiring a tough, lean-and-mean manager is a part of this approach, which usually produces some undesirable effects as well as desirable ones. A cleaver may cut out a lot of muscle as well as fat. Parts of the organization which should be expanded to develop new and profitable lines of business may be cut along with the nonproductive areas.

When costs get out of line for the whole organization, it's the function of top management to decide that a fixed percentage of reduction will take place, but this doesn't necessarily mean that such cuts will be uniform across the board. Rather, the details of where the ax will fall should be worked out at second and third levels to assure that maximum savings and minimum damage occur.

Lee Iacocca found on taking over at Chrysler that he had to make drastic cutbacks to save the company and satisfy creditors. His response was to establish an "equality of sacrifice" rule, which meant that everyone would hurt a little and that he would take a pay cut first before asking the union and officers to take pay cuts. Yet it was his decision that a certain amount would be cut; it wasn't a decision made by popular vote.

2. A Hiring Freeze

Another of the most common methods for cutting back on white-collar jobs is for top management to place a freeze on all new hires, even replacements for those who quit. This approach uses the normal turnover that occurs in any organization to reduce the work force and save labor costs.

Consultant Mike Kami, a provocative speaker, often shocks business audiences by suggesting that firing fifty executives will improve productivity in most firms. The effect is similar when you put a freeze on replacements and force people in management to examine carefully whether or not every position is really necessary.

This scheme places a heavy burden of detail on top people, who get flooded with "emergency hiring" requests when somebody quits. It works best when you prepare a list of crucial and vital positions for which replacements will be approved and then place the burden of proof for other positions on the people filing the requests.

Developmental programs and activities are those most likely to get hurt by a hiring freeze. It takes darn good management to make a freeze rule work for the long-term benefit of the organization.

3. Early Retirements

An early retirement program is still another popular method for trimming white-collar ranks. This substitutes a one-time lump payment for fixed labor costs in the future. You sweeten up the retirement package, and if people buy into it your labor costs will decline immediately. Whether the labor savings exceeds the cost in the first year isn't the crucial issue. It is getting the size of the staff down so that the future looks rosier.

Early retirement programs usually involve two distinct elements:

a. You try to make all such retirements voluntary. Get a legal document to this effect signed by the retiree, thus avoiding any possibility of lawsuits for age discrimination or for wrongful firing under "at will" firing laws.

b. You create an outplacement department to assist retirees and actively represent those who want to find new jobs. Assistance includes personal counseling, career advice, resume writing, and active job search efforts among potential employers.

4. Tougher Performance Appraisals

One of the tangible effects of drives to improve white-collar productivity has been a tightening of the screws on performance ratings. It's recognized that if a separation is challenged, the performance review records may be subpoenaed and the judge will review the entire plan for fairness. As a result there is new emphasis on rating performance accurately, especially unsatisfactory performance.

As everyone realizes, it is easier to give a favorable performance rating that a critical one. You are apt to get arguments and protests when you call bad performance bad performance, so the path of least resistance is to rate everyone high.

Like the forward pass in football, which can be caught, dropped, or intercepted, a performance appraisal system can do three things, two of which are bad. A good system can help you to sort out good performance from bad. A poor system does nothing to justify a firing decision and can also get you into legal trouble. Old-fashioned but still widely used personality trait assessments or other subjective standards cannot be relied upon to weed out bad performance, nor are they defensible in court.

5. Substituting Equipment for People

The recent enormous growth in the use of computers, data processing equipment, and word processors is largely due to the search for savings in wages and salaries for clerical employees. The paperless "office of the future" is possible today, and it's quite predictable that further labor-saving economies will arrive with a vengeance during the rest of the decade.

Substituting equipment for people isn't really as cost-effective as the salespeople would have you believe. Computer experts state it quite plainly: Don't expect to save money by buying a computer. You may save some on labor costs, but the biggest gain from computers is to be found in getting more useful information for your business or organization. Nevertheless, most managers under the gun to cut costs and improve white-collar productivity are apt to move strongly toward buying hardware—some would say toys—to produce a short-term reduction in white-collar salaries while moving expenses to the capital budgets and overhead costs.

Most substitutions of equipment for people are systems changes, not an approach to human efficiency. The drive for white-collar productivity promises to be a complete systems revolution, of which equipment and capital infusion is a detail.

6. Better Productivity Measures

For more than five decades factories have concentrated upon standards of performance and work measurement, but the application of that same scientific approach to white-collar jobs simply has not followed at the same pace. In more offices than not, the methods employed in doing work have been left to the person doing the job. The result is a hodgepodge of methods, some of which are efficient and most of which are not. The idea that standards of performance can be established for white-collar occupations has made some progress in routine clerical operations, but the more difficult areas are those where the jobs are technical and professional, and where they show considerable variation from day to day. Here the best approach might be to tighten up position descriptions.

The productivity of white-collar workers cannot be measured without the active and full cooperation of the jobholder. If workers have a good reason to avoid such measurement—such as hearty distrust of the boss and the reasons for the measurement—the whole process goes down the tube. Given a reason to cooperate, most workers could help to produce some excellent and useful productivity measures.

7. Job Enrichment and MBO

If the white-collar workers themselves desire to improve the way things are done, they may prove to be a superior source of improvement. The involvement of employees in job design is the basic idea underlying job enrichment programs. Job design means grouping tasks together into more effective sets of duties. It begins with interviews of employees to find out what they do, how they do it, where their work comes from and where it goes, how quality is checked, and what they like and dislike about their jobs. The distinctive feature of job enrichment is that it attacks the factors that employees dislike, by giving them responsibility for final output and by allowing them both to check their own work and to make routine decisions.

MBO is a relatively untried approach for the improvement of white-collar performance. While most major firms use MBO for sales and manufacturing, where outputs are most easily counted, its application in clerical- and professional-level occupations is quite limited. In brief, MBO requires every manager and subordinate to sit down at the beginning of every year and talk out the objectives of the subordinate's job. The product of this two-way dialogue is a memorandum confirming agreements made on goals, standards, and results sought.

8. Team Building and Quality Circles

Because of the complexity of chores performed by white-collar workers, it isn't surprising that some people are engaged in mutually exclusive tasks while others let certain things fall between the chairs and remain undone. The process of team building and the creation of quality circles, both of which programs are usually aided by a consultant or development specialist, can be effective in overcoming these problems. At their best, quality circles are group meetings of people whose work is related, and the end result is problem-solving. Chronic concerns about quality, cost, volume, time, and interpersonal relations can be effectively ironed out by the people who know the real nature of the problems and who have some reality-based information on their causes.

9. The White-Collar Productivity Committee

When white-collar productivity is crucial to the organization, it is common to have a committee which decides that programs will be undertaken. The committee usually includes systems experts, MIS staff people, managerial accountants, and human resources staff people, the higher in rank the better. This group makes judgments about cost reduction programs, tracks actual results against goals, and issues periodic reports. The white-collar productivity committee also has to be concerned with program overload, which occurs when too many new programs are started and pushed too fast, putting so much pressure on everyone that nothing constructive gets achieved.

Part IV
The
Superior–Subordinate
Relationship

The man who trusts other men will make fewer mistakes than he who distrusts them.

—C.D. Cavour

13
Mentoring: The Tool
for Integrating Management

To puff and get oneself puffed have become different branches of a new profession.

—Anthony Trollope

Two Demands of Integration

The system by which the goals of the employee are integrated with the goals of the organization is the basis not only for individual personal growth but also for supplying talent for higher-level responsibility. When an executive talks to a subordinate about the job, its requirements and its challenges, the talk is developmental and not just company business. It's true that an organization has to have people who will work at its tasks and make commitments to its objectives. The relationship, however, is broader than simply shoptalk. It has two major dimensions:

1. *It must be functional.* The boss has a lot of work which has to be done, goods to be manufactured and sold, paper to be processed, plans to be devised, problems to be solved, opportunities to be exploited. These are the functions of the business, and from the boss's view the benefits of setting goals with subordinates is that these functions will be done on time, at suitable quality, and within costs which are more or less predictable. Even a selfish boss can agree that if goal setting produces better results for the business, it is advantageous to engage in such a process. It is most likely that the high acceptance rate of MBO and similar processes as a management system has been exactly for this reason; it gets the job done.

Goal setting isn't an additional program nor an incidental side effect in the management job. It is a way of doing it better. Any inconveniences which it appears to impose are more than amply returned. As the Iacocca story reveals, goal setting is a means of turning around sick organizations. It is a means of getting problems defined in the form of objectives which are embedded in the job content of a responsible person committed to their solution. The prediction of exact outcomes in such areas as research or staff work isn't always possible. But the likelihood of success attending efforts in those areas is higher when people who must produce innovation are personally committed to an outcome within a time and cost budget. It is a fine tuning of the ancient principle of organization known as division of labor.

2. *It is developmental of subordinates.* From the perspective of the subordinate, goals-centered management, wherein boss and subordinate sit down and mutually agree upon job responsibilities, goals, priorities, and plans for getting there, produces personal growth in competence. The contract-like relationship demands commitments which might not have been made without such a dialogue.

When I set forth to negotiate goals with my boss I have created a new quasi need which has considerable power to affect my behavior. It is this commitment to new behavior which causes me to grow, to stretch my capacity, and to challenge myself to do better things than I have done in the past. At the same time the organization gains, I too have some distinct gains. Even if I am an utterly selfish person whose major concern is meeting my own needs, when I am challenged and make commitments I become something bigger, better, more competent, and more capable of independent action.

This element of increased freedom for subordinates is an often-overlooked benefit of contracting commitments with a boss. I am committing myself to an output or outcome for a specific time period and, within the limit of law and policy, can take whatever actions I choose to get there.

The chance, even the obligation, to talk to a boss on a planned, regular, formal basis about the future in one's work is a precious experience for people who seek more responsibility, greater challenge, a better paying position, higher status, and the chance to make a significant contribution. The failure which comes from not knowing what was expected has been removed from my job. I know my status and my function.

The Importance of Mentoring

While there are of course cases where younger people direct older ones, the reverse is more common. The experience and wider knowledge of the higher levels is an ordinary condition in most organizations. The necessity of having that accumulated experience passed on to newer, younger, and less experienced persons is an organizational imperative. The organization with no memories fails to capture the experience of its own past and is doomed to repeat its mistakes again and again. Even more important, the need to have superior-ranking persons see to the growth and development of lesser-ranking people is a chronic concern. Young people who must puff themselves up in order to move upward suffer a severe disadvantage. Far better is the advice of the writer of Proverbs: "Let another man praise thee, and not thine own mouth." How can a boss praise and recommend a subordinate without firsthand information about how well that subordinate has done in setting goals, making commitments to their solution, and then matching words with actions?

This relationship, beyond the functional and developmental goals of a boss and a subordinate each pursuing their own separate interests, has a joining quality that is greater than the sum of the two motives of the two parties. Rather than a zero–sum game or a win–lose contest between organization and individual, it is a win–win game which produces benefits for both.

B.C. Forbes, the publisher, once said that "despite the organization of industry to make routine labor automatic, every individual must be a boss in the application of his personal energies to the task at hand." When this principle is applied systematically, many minor managers who wasted their time directing the detailed behavior of their underlings can achieve real executive caliber. They can limit their bossiness to coordinating each worker's task with the efforts of the entire organization.

When the goals of the individual are integrated with those of the organization, a higher level of personal relationship emerges, for the boss becomes more helper than judge. Such practices as driving people, snooping upon them as they work, demanding endless explanations, second-guessing, and looking over their shoulders can be set aside for a healthier and more productive relationship. The goals provide standards which must be met, and the control element of the job becomes largely one of inspecting and checking results against targets rather than policing conformity to rules which may or may not be related to the results being sought.

This relationship of helping is sometimes known as mentoring. It is grounded in a joint understanding or objective between boss and subordinate. *Mentor* was the name of a servant of the Greek king Odysseus, who, when he left for the wars, instructed his servant to take charge of the education and rearing of his son Telemachus. Mentor was charged with the objective of teaching Telemachus not only the knowledge in books but also "the wiles of the world."

It is exactly this attention to the wiles of the world that an immediate boss has the greatest opportunity to teach when he or she acts as a mentor. Most organizations have a culture—sometimes known as "the ropes"—which must be observed if one is to rise and avoid the errors of inappropriate behavior in the process. Learning the ways that decisions get made, who makes what decisions, how issues get identified, and how they get resolved are part of the ropes. The boss relates external and internal facts to identify the critical issues facing the organization at the moment. These critical issues shape the requirements which organizations make of their people, and the boss is the best source for identifying critical issues for those below him in rank.

Relationships are always a critical issue in an organization. Information about who is the strongest executive and who is out of favor may be transmitted only by word of mouth. What corporate or organizational strategies are highest in urgency is often another such subject.

The mentor both gives and receives information. From the subordinate he learns his capabilities and needs, wishes and ambitions, and is in a suitable position to assist in growing people's larger capabilities.

Mentoring Is Distinctively American

It's a habit of many consultants, writers, and academics these days to attribute all kinds of magical qualities to foreign management systems. Where it used to be the German Miracle twenty years ago and then the Swedish system ten years ago, today many people are enamored with the Japanese management system. But if it's a model of managerial excellence that we're looking for, I would suggest that there are numerous features of American management strategies which are distinctively ours and which can become the basis of our own renewal. The search for excellence, which is the message of a best-seller by Thomas Peters and Robert Waterman, Jr., is a worthwhile focus for management development.

Certainly one of the more distinctively American management practices is the way in which senior managers coach their subordinates. Call it mentoring, coaching, counseling, or the "understudy method" of supervision. In more tradition-bound cultures only a few elite young people—overwhelmingly males—have the benefit of personal coaching from the senior people in power. In most nations of the world today, the children of the upper classes are far more likely to be those chosen for special mentoring by the ruling group. But in America, and perhaps in Canada, talented young people from all levels of society may find doors open for them to move into corporate management and to enjoy the benefits of mentoring by the present leaders. The child of the workingman, taxi driver, or clerk can find his or her way to executive row with the assistance of a senior authority figure.

Most managers can readily name the person who was most responsible for their first move up the ladder. For some it was a schoolteacher, uncle, or neighbor. Yet the most important mentor for the most successful managers was an early boss who stirred up an ambition to rise in the organization, who assured them that they really had more talent than they were using, or who convinced them that the negative assessment of their peers was wrong and that they were right about their own abilities. For others, the big career boost came at a later stage when they were given a special assignment or membership on a special task force which opened their eyes to possibilities they hadn't previously imagined.

Choosing a Mentor

Choosing a mentor isn't exactly like hiring a new secretary or choosing a mate. The choice is often accidental. Some people have nurturing parents who spend a lot of time helping their kids grow. Others don't. The same is true of bosses. Some are people builders and others are people shrinkers. Some bosses habitually work at putting down the best hopes and aspirations of their subordinates, advising them that they are foolish and presumptuous in even considering being anything more than they are right now. All of us can recall such a person in our past who scoffed or sneered at our hopes. The key to finding your personal mentor is to get away from the scoffer and to get close to the person who cheers you on.

Your mentor may be your boss, but this is not necessarily so. Bosses are in a natural position to coach and encourage people, but many are too busy or are not disposed to mentor their subordinates. For one thing, they may hesitate to show special attention to a single employee. For another, they may see and fear your potential to rise above them. However, the most natural mentor and the easiest to get in tune with is your own boss, if he or she is a developmental and people-building type of person.

Your mentor might be another manager or highly placed person with whom your work contacts are occasional and casual but who has been favorably impressed with your work and your potential. A mentoring relationship is an unofficial relationship which just happens to develop; you can't sign somebody up for a two-year mentoring contract. You talk to your mentor occasionally, usually about business, but then extend the discussion to ask for advice beyond the immediate concern.

Your mentor must be a successful person, at least to the extent that he or she is a model for you to aspire to. This doesn't rule out a supervisor mentoring a worker even if this mentor may never get beyond the supervisory level. The important thing is that at the time of the mentoring relationship, the mentor is above his or her understudy. People may outgrow a mentor and need to find a new one at a higher level.

What does a good mentor do that produces development and growth? Business history shows that the best bosses were people with a strong goal orientation. The major lesson they imparted was that success comes from remitting attention to purposes and a drive to achieve goals.

This is not to suggest that all such people worked with a formal MBO program. On the contrary, the managerial style of the best mentors is characterized by a goal-centered orientation, not by formal procedures or a set of forms. A mentor imparts his or her own best skills by example, by rewarding and punishing, by setting standards for people, by showing confidence, and by leaving people alone while they are working.

Five Qualities of Good Mentors

If you work for a good mentor, your learning centers around goals, expectations, standards, and the pressure to do all that you are capable of doing. The best mentors are characterized by these five qualities:

1. They are superior performers in their own jobs. One doesn't pick a loser to imitate.

2. They realize that they are setting an example and behave in such a way that their behavior is worth imitating.

3. They are supportive and helpful of subordinates in the performance of their jobs, but avoid usurping their jobs or insisting upon things being done exactly their way.

4. They are good delegators. That is, they let people know what results are expected, give them help and support, and then leave them alone while they are working toward those goals.

5. They arrange feedback so that their people can know how well they are doing in the job while they are actually doing

it. This makes people into self-rewarders and self-punishers and teaches them to work under self-control.

Mentoring is a philosophy as well as a set of techniques. Good mentors are people who have a healthy relationship toward others. They assume that people have greater capacities than they are presently using and work hard at bringing out whatever latent talent is there. While this attitude is obviously good for the subordinate, the mentor knows that this is not a wholly selfless system. The manager who works at bringing out the best in his or her people will benefit from improved organizational performance, increased productivity, and a high level of excellence in operations.

Although the practice of mentoring is widespread, it isn't commonplace. There are still many people in top positions who regard their subordinates as a resource to be exploited. The bad mentor is one who sees subordinates as competitors who must be put down, or who takes the detached view of demanding a fair day's work for a fair day's pay and pays no attention to the development of his or her people.

Such attitudes do nothing for people building. You can't be exacting, hostile, judgmental, or punitive in dealing with subordinates if you hope to elicit their best abilities. You can't act in such a way that people who see you at work at your executive tasks might conclude that you lack a caring attitude, or that you regard subordinates as objects to be used like a Kleenex and disposed of when no longer useful.

To extend a caring attitude to organizational policy levels calls for standards of performance which demand the development of people. Performance appraisals of managers and objectives for senior executives must include some considerations of how many people have been promoted out of a particular unit to bigger jobs. Managers in high-turnover organizations who never produce high-quality people for the rest of the organization are doing only a fraction of their job. "What are you doing to develop people under your charge?" should be a required question for every performance review.

Firms such as IBM, General Electric, and DuPont clearly have a people-growing orientation. What makes this clear is the fact that they produce more than enough managers internally for their own growth needs.

Problems Relating to Sex, Race, and Ethnic Origin

Differences in sex and race between a mentor and a subordinate can hinder the mentoring relationship. Many a senior male executive would agree that speculation about the possibility of a more personal relationship with a young woman is to be avoided. The notoriety of the Bendix case involving Bill Agee and his protege, Mary Cunningham, has done a lot to dampen the prospects for many young and talented women to find a mentor. The same problems exist, of course, in the mentoring relationship between a female executive and a young man. But if all the contacts are taking place within a controlled environment, such as the home office, and during regular working hours, it may be possible for an executive to serve as a good mentor to a young person of the opposite sex.

When there is a difference of race between mentor and protege, the problem of external opinion doesn't have nearly as much effect. In fact, it may be construed as desirable for today's generation to take on a young black or other minority individual as a protege, but this is still a problem for many senior managers. Until they have learned to be comfortable with a person of a different race, many older managers are awkward with such people and even then do well as mentors only with people of the same sex and those whose manners and values are consistent with their own. Many young minority executives have found that they do better in getting the support of senior members of the establishment if they are seen as being "really quite like us."

The personal values of some potential white male mentors have an important bearing upon their willingness to coach, sponsor, and tutor a young hispanic or a woman. There are those whose social views are such that they simply can't see themselves having anything to do with such a person. For others, there is a strong bias toward people from their own religious, ethnic, or cultural background. In one large firm it was an article of faith among younger managers that "you gotta be Italian to get ahead around here." In others, you won't stand much chance of being mentored by a senior officer unless you went to a certain college, received a certain degree, or were born in a certain part of the country. Such barriers are fortunately on the decline, but a certain amount of personal bias does still enter into the choice of proteges.

Faced with opposition from potential mentors, women and minorities have turned to informal and voluntary support groups, networking, and caucuses instead of looking for a single mentor. This approach has several advantages. For one thing, a group provides psychological support as well as practical learning. For another, a group provides feedback and counseling on personal behavior and dress, and on dealing with discrimination and organizational policies which block women and minorities from getting where they want to go. But even more important, groups often invite senior executives to visit. During such visits the group's members gain the benefits of mentoring from senior officers in an environment that is both developmental and nonthreatening.

Ethical Issues in Mentoring

Another important problem area in mentoring involves ethical issues. There is no formal set of rules of conduct for the informal mentoring relationship, but some commonsense guides should be followed:

1. Don't show favoritism and call it mentoring. There are people we like and people we don't like, but you can't use rank to reward your friends and punish your enemies in choosing the people you will help to get ahead in the organization.

2. Don't let a group of "crown princes" emerge who are apparently destined for a fast ride to the top. Make the mentoring relationship a temporary one, reviewed annually and based upon continued excellence of performance. If the individual lets his or her visibility as a protege get in the way of doing the job supremely well, it is time to terminate the mentoring relationship.

3. Don't demand and extract gratitude in the form of repayment from a protege. This includes personal services, including sexual favors, in return for career assistance. A recent article in *Har-*

per's noted that, in a majority of cases, women with older male mentors engage in sexual relations with their mentor. This is devastating to the morale and confidence of the rest of the help. Gratitude on the part of the protege is to be expressed by helping somebody else later on.

4. Be sure that your proteges are worthy of the special advice and assistance you are giving. You can't afford to push ahead people who are unworthy.

5. It is best to have two or more proteges at a time. This avoids the charge of favoritism.

6. The only solid basis for mentoring is to provide opportunity and incentive. The proteges must do the rest on their own.

Mentoring Managers in Their Thirties

People in their twenties are often seen as immature, narcissistic, self-obsessed, concerned with pleasure, and unwilling to defer gratifications. People in their thirties, on the other hand, need to make some important decisions and it's vital for employers to help people through this period of their lives. If people haven't made a mark by the time they are forty, that's a sign for many large firms that their future progress may be limited.

Most major managerial career patterns will be shaped during a person's thirties. Either you'll get locked into a career as a manufacturing, sales, or accounting specialist, or you'll get yourself marked as a bright and rising star. This can be a time of exhilaration and achievement, or it can be a time of disillusionment. The rising level of discontent in middle management is often rooted in the malaise and disappointment that comes with being in your thirties and realizing that you probably won't ever become president or even a vice president of your firm.

Let's suppose that you are mentoring a thirty-year-old manager and want to be sure that whatever talent he or she has will be fully used. How do you go about doing this? Or suppose you are a thirty-year-old and want to continue to rise and not become a shelf-sitter. What are the key events and attitudes which can make or break your aspirations?

1. *You can get marked as a star.* People acquire most of their reputations during their thirties, so if you're to get labeled as having high potential, this is the time for that to happen. Once labeled as a rising star, you'll find avenues open, opportunities presented, contacts made, and challenges offered which will really give you a crack at joining the fast risers. Some of this reputation is carried over from your twenties when you were working in the salt mines as a salesperson, foreman, or junior-level supervisor. Mistakes from the past will be forgotten, along with your brilliant college record. You must now start delivering some exceptional results in the face of uncertainty and tough competition. This is the time when you get a chance at some really important jobs in which results can't be concealed under the bureaucratic red tape and controls of lower rank. Lee Iacocca became general manager of the Ford Division and developed the Mustang while in his thirties, thus assuring his future role in the corporate world.

2. *You can lose your dreams.* Far more people will level off during their thirties than will get labeled as having star potential. Often this comes with being passed over for a job, or appearing to be trapped in a dead-end job in an out-of-the-way location. It's such times that cause many thirty-year-olds to lose their dreams. "I need $30,000 a year to meet my obligations" is a golden handcuff shackling many people in their thirties to the sure path, keeping them, for instance, from the risky path of starting their own business where the big success lies.

3. *You can lose your ambitions.* During your late thirties you attend the twentieth reunion of your high school class and find that someone you used to look down upon now owns a string of transmission shops and drives a top-of-the-line Mercedes while you're still driving a four-year-old Toyota. Or you find yourself working under someone who is several years younger than yourself. Or you make a big mistake which smashes your reputation like a torpedo at the waterline and for months afterward people are patronizing you and standing around the watercooler talking about your fall. The wiseacres write you off. But then comes the really important event: you write yourself off. You begin to rationalize that you don't want that big job anyhow. "The old rat race" becomes a standard phrase in your speech. You spend more and more time with other

people who have lost their ambitions. Your self-esteem peters out and you settle for small victories and local triumphs.

4. *You may become distraught over the loss of youth.* People in their thirties begin to realize the inexorable nature of aging. You get bifocals and discover that your suit size is now a 44 Regular instead of the trim-cut 40 that you used to wear. Your hair thins and you begin to see the first traces of gray around the edges, and then you look with dismay at some old photographs of yourself taken just after you graduated from college. Your tennis game is more cerebral than agile and you don't join liberal crusades like you used to. Untimely strains and sprains make you more conscious of aging, and you fight back only sporadically and without much success.

5. *You may become more family oriented than work oriented.* By the time you're in your mid-thirties your kids are well into school and you begin to project your future through the opportunities you can create for them. Your spouse may also have a career and you can't be as mobile as when you operated solo. You can't accept promotions that involve a transfer unless you can find a suitable spot for your spouse as well. Time management becomes more important as the pressures of family responsibility begin to press into job time. When two parents are working, dividing up the housework and the children's affairs becomes a job for the professional traffic manager, and fitting in crucial small duties becomes a job for a time expert with enormous planning ability.

6. *You may experience separation anxiety.* The demands of spouses, children, unreasonable bosses, aging parents, and social needs create a web of tensions which produce a sense of powerlessness. The response for many people may be to grab a new job which holds out a momentary promise of brightness or a higher salary which seems to be a godsend. Or it may be to get a divorce and reach out for a younger and more vivacious sexual companion who seems to promise none of the tensions of the old ties that bind. Separation itself produces anxiety and, occasionally, a loss of self-esteem. In the worst cases this leads to bitterness, disappointment, and disillusionment.

7. *You may become resistant to change.* With fifteen or twenty years of work life behind you, you cite the virtues and glories of the

past more often. You tell more war stories about the good old days. You tend to see every change as being nothing more than a rehash of things you have seen before. ("We had quality circles back in the early seventies, but we didn't call them that.") You find yourself resenting the brashness of people in their twenties and talk to them in an avuncular fashion. You become more sensitive to competition from younger people and to their eternal optimism and inexperience. You put a lot of energy into devising arguments against things you don't like, including things that are new and novel. You become more enamored of tradition and precedent. Your bad habits become charming idiosyncrasies (in your mind) and you take pride in your shortcomings and limitations. ("I never could do math.")

8. *You may put emphasis on affiliations instead of achievements.* As challenges and opportunities decline, you center your attentions on affiliations. ("Sure I know Mr. Big. We go way back. I call him Bill.") More and more conversations turn on contacts and connections. You become zealous in striking up and maintaining affiliations with those in power, seeking to share in their power vicariously.

9. *You may master the put-down.* Starting with your kids, and then on the job with subordinates, you may pay a bit too much attention to the arts of domination and intimidation, perhaps in an attempt to find satisfaction in whatever small power you can muster in place of the higher levels of real power which you have missed. As a veteran of the organization, the manager in his or her thirties has mastered the ropes and become the model bureaucrat. There is a temptation to display that mastery. ("I can't accept this because the signature is on the wrong line. Do it over.")

10. *You may master the art of criticism.* As experience becomes a basis for making judgments, there is a tendency for managers in their thirties to clutch their work tightly to their breasts and to redo the work of their subordinates to add all the right touches. It's possible to become especially critical of superiors whose shortcomings are now more clearly seen than when you were young and idealistic. Cynicism may become a habit.

All ten of these events and attitudes are natural evolutions from early experience, and some of them are traps which keep people from becoming stars and rising to their full potential. Aside from merely avoiding the traps, however, managers in their thirties need some positive elements in their career-planning strategies for supplanting those traps and keeping them from growing into dominant behavior.

Career Advice for Thirty-year-olds

Here are some positive guides for career planning for managers in their thirties.

Keep Pursuing Your Dream

There are numerous examples of people who were bogged down at thirty and forty who made it big in their fifties and sixties. Clement Stone, the founder of Combined Insurance Companies of America, kept his dream of success alive although he didn't really make it big until his sixties. The reason that one's thirties are crucial is that this is the time when the dreams of many people die.

Set High Goals and Then Plan How to Reach Them

The lessons of business history are clear: people who make it big in the world of business do so because of a goal and a plan. If you aim low, you'll achieve little. If you aim high, however, you may miss a few times but you may eventually accomplish your goal. Having a long-term goal as well as some immediate targets is part of the process. If the long-term goal remains in place, the immediate setbacks and failures won't seem quite so important.

Start where you are with an honest assessment of your situation and match that against your long-term objective. Then every decision you make can be one that moves you toward your ultimate goal. Most people who lose their vision level off and turn to complaining about their troubles and disappointments.

Develop the Practice of Self-Command

Thomas Schelling of Harvard recently delivered a lecture to a sophisticated audience of economic theorists and social scientists in which he proposed that "self-command is an important principle in economic policy and rational choice." Anticipatory self-command, according to Schelling, means that people are in evident possession of their faculties, know what they are talking about, and will rationally seek to compel or alter their own subsequent behavior. We do this, for example, when we swear off smoking and instruct all of the people around us not to give us a cigarette when we ask for one, or when we ask our friends at a party not to let us drive home if we've had too much to drink. The idea is that human beings can issue self-commands in advance of a situation in which they might engage in behavior contrary to their best interests.

Schelling suggests that there are numerous forms of self-command which have a lot of relevance to the career-oriented young manager: Relinquish your authority to goof off to somebody else; make a commitment or contract to do better; remove yourself from the wrong path; remove the temptations and mischievous resources which lead you astray from pursuing your own dream and goal; appoint a watchdog to check you; arrange penalties and rewards; reschedule your life to make the right path part of your lifestyle; identify the trigger mechanisms which set off wrong behavior, and control those mechanisms by anticipation.

Self-commands frequently involve a voluntary commitment to another person or group, and in this way they are rather similar to the practice of management by objectives. In making a commitment to your boss to pursue some project or goal, you are exercising a form of what Schelling calls self-command. You didn't really have to make that advance commitment. You might have talked yourself into doing something that would have been easier. But your promise now becomes a form of self-command.

Set Some Personal Development Objectives for Yourself

No subordinate in his or her thirties should be allowed to escape with stating only routine, problem-solving, and innovative objectives. Every goals statement for the career-oriented subordinate should include some personal development objectives. What will you do to improve your own capacities and abilities? What challenges will you set for yourself? What kinds of courses or readings will prepare you for these new challenges? What will you need to know and be able to do to succeed in your aspirations? What will you do about each of these in the coming year?

Career-oriented managers in their thirties are really at a cross-roads. There are two selves, one which would become a superstar and the other which would become a shelf-sitter. Putting the potential shelf-sitter under self-command can be made easier by some personal development objectives and some solid mentoring by an understanding boss.

14
Commitment: The Tie That Binds

Intentional action is first a motivation process; second an act of choice
or decision of intentions; and third is the action itself.
—Kurt Lewin

P eople who have intentions are committed to the completion of
some kind of result, or to an action which might lead to results.
It begins with some kind of motive, or a choice of motives. Maybe
the employee could go to the watercooler, could work hard, could
turn in his or her resignation, could withhold a new idea which
would benefit the employer. At first all options are open. Should I
get an MBA, go to law school, get a transfer to the sales department, join the Peace Corps, or have an Egg McMuffin? The choices
that could be made range from the most immediate and trivial to
the vital and life-altering.

In such an ambivalent state I don't have any commitments, for
I haven't yet made up my mind. The only common element is that
I have common drives with other humans: I need recognition, belonging, security, adequacy, and the like. I also have some *acquired*
motives which are secondary and not instinctive or basic in pressing
me. The avoidance of danger, the need to eat when I'm hungry,
drink when I'm thirsty, and so forth aren't something I had to study
to learn; I was born that way.

Most of the behavior we expect of people in organizations isn't
instinctive. Nobody was born with the instinct to be a salesperson
or an engineer or to pilot a combat aircraft. There may be some
instinctive behavior which must be employed in such work, but the
choice of such an occupation, and the specific goals which are required to succeed in it, is an acquired drive or a "quasi need," as
Kurt Lewin called it.

Life in the civilized world of organizations is made up of a whole structure of quasi needs. These quasi needs are the electives which the employee can bring to a job. For some people in lower economic strata with a dire need for income, it may be the fear of losing the job which produces the intention to get up and go to work each day. *Question:* "How long have you worked here?" *Answer:* "Since the day they threatened to fire me."

In high-level technical, managerial, and professional fields where there are often other alternatives to working for one specific organization, this kind of fear as the motivator is far less likely to dominate. More likely the quasi needs for high-level workers involve the need for social acceptance, ego gratification, or the expression of creative talents. At the same time it is possible that there may be multiple ways of producing satisfaction of these quasi needs, and that is the root of intentional behavior.

The individual chooses to meet his or her basic needs by creating certain quasi needs and intentions within the framework of a job, profession, or occupation. The employer will benefit most when the quasi needs chosen by the employee also help attain the objectives of the organization for profit, service, growth, efficiency, productivity, and the like.

Is Integration of Needs Possible?

Many traditional bosses start out with some assumptions which treat employee needs in unitary, single-need fashion. This assumes that while the organization has many needs, the employee has but one, or two at most, usually safety and security. "A fair day's work for a fair day's pay" is the ancient adage which describes this bargain in traditional employment practices.

The joint setting of goals between boss and subordinate starts with some different assumptions:

1. The employee is free to define a wide range of different intentions, some of which will be more useful to the employer than others.

2. The selection of those intentions is under the control of the employee. I may choose to "do the work which is put before

me," as Henry Ford, Sr., defined the worker's job. Or I may choose to do more, or something differently, or refrain from doing something with the effect that the organization will benefit more greatly.

3. While it has been argued by Lewin that the need to set quasi needs, that is, the need to set goals, is instinctive, the actual choice of specific needs is determined by the situation within which I work.

The joint discussion of objectives with subordinates, then, is the psychological process of defining goals to maximize benefits to the organization while it satisfies the quasi needs of the employee.

The Importance of Commitment

Even though I may have a strong basic urge to set goals and pursue them to completion by action, such an urge doesn't ordinarily become reality on the job until I make a commitment to somebody else whose opinion is important to me. This process, which Robert House has called Management by Commitment, produces an integration which should in all probability meet the needs of both. Internally, commitment means that I have chosen my intentions and will be unsatisfied until they are turned into completed action. Externally these commitments resemble contracts at law.

At ITT, reports Charles MacDonald, the system known in some firms as MBO is known as Management by Contract. Both employer and employee negotiate an agreement which satisfies the needs of both: of the employer for productivity, quality, and the like; and of the employee to complete his or her intentions. A contract under law is a "legally enforceable agreement between two or more persons involving mutual promises to do or not to do something." Some contracts are oral, but are nonetheless binding.

Objectives negotiated with an organization or a boss are most enforceable if there is a consideration on both sides. Those who attain their objectives will be rewarded within the system of merit pay, bonuses, promotion schemes, and the like by the employer. What are some of the parallel features of goal setting in organizations and legal contracts?

1. They are agreed upon by both parties.

2. There must be a consideration.

3. The objective to be achieved must be lawful.

4. The contract must require specific performance within an agreed time period.

5. The parties must be able to deliver that which they promise.

Once the contract or commitment is made, the parties are required to exercise due diligence in performing. The exact motions and course for achieving the performance aren't necessarily spelled out. If I contract to deliver a new television set to your house for $200, it doesn't matter whether I deliver by truck, car, or dogsled, or pack it on my back. The contract is for performance, not method, as long as the method is legal. I can't contract for somebody else's behavior, and I can't breach a contract by idle or fraudulent changes without going back to the other party for agreement. The integration of our mutual needs is thus confirmed by mutually negotiated agreement for specific performance of results, and confirmed in writing by both sides.

A contract is discharged when the terms of the contract are performed by both sides. If the organization agrees to some objectives, and in turn agrees upon a budget needed to complete it, both sides must deliver performance. This reduces the flexibility of the boss to second-guess, exercise hindsight, or refuse to follow the terms of the contract by failing to deliver the consideration agreed upon. When the U.S. Congress established a goals-setting program for awarding bonuses to senior civil servants in the 1979 Civil Service Reform Act, then reneged on paying the agreed-upon bonuses, it breached the contract.

A commitment between a boss and subordinate can be discharged by amendment when the parties agree to the substitution of a new contract. You agree to hatch a dozen eggs for your boss, but learn later that the eggs were in fact hard-boiled prior to the contract's being negotiated. It would be only sensible to negotiate a new agreement. One side, however, is not free to break the commitment unilaterally simply because it is too hard or too inconvenient, or because of second thoughts. Breach of commitment thus consists of any unjustified failure to perform the terms of the commitment. Such a breach may be full or partial, and the extent of remedy which the parties might invoke will be based upon the damage done by the failure.

In short, commitment isn't simply a psychological condition within the individual. Commitment in such a definition is certainly a psychological condition, showing serious intention to take some action or deliver some specific performance, and is internalized by the individual. The commitment which becomes public and binding is the one to which both sides agree through negotiation and confirmation in writing, resembling a performance contract.

Turn an Ordinary Job into a Great One

Abraham Lincoln once said that most people are about as happy as they make up their minds to be. That's true to a large degree about people at work. There are people who make $100,000 a year who are miserable, and others who make $10,000 a year who are pleased as punch about their situation in life. Admittedly it's easier to be happy when you're rich and healthy than when you're poor and sick, but there are elements in every job which can make it a great job or a hell on earth.

Figuring out what makes an ordinary job a great one would be useful for those millions of people who pile into their cars every Monday morning with a sense of loathing, dread, distaste, or boredom. Knowing how to turn an ordinary job into something exciting and fulfilling for people is an immense asset which some managers possess and others don't.

It's my observation that, more often than not, the people who find that they have great jobs are those who are committed to their jobs. That of course leaves unanswered the question of whether it's the intrinsic greatness of the job that produces the commitment, or the commitment that makes the job great. Nonetheless, people who are committed to something find that money, time, drudgery, pain, and even terror don't really make the job bad. Their commitment overrides the disadvantages.

Bosses who can generate commitment to the purposes of the

organization get better results than people who merely pay a fair day's wage for a fair day's work.

There are two distinct elements in commitment. The first is the actual set of promises, made to somebody whose opinion is considered important, to produce some outcome or product by a specific time, the certainty of which may be low or unclear. The second element is the internalizing of those promises, so that a promise made to somebody else becomes a promise to yourself.

The achievement of doing what we set out to do is self-rewarding. It's often the beauty or nobility of the job itself that produces the internal commitment.

Regardless of whether commitment is self-created or a product of a management style, the committed person is distinctively different from the uncommitted or less committed individual:

1. Committed people have high levels of acceptance for themselves and others. They know who they are and they like themselves. They accept the fallibility of others without dismay, and they accept their own good and bad qualities without being self-punishers. They don't accept guile, phoniness, false front, sham, bunkum, and protective coloration in themselves or in others, but they do accept natural qualities without worrying about them.

2. Committed people are more spontaneous than less committed people. They're willing to plunge into something after due consideration of the risks. They accept new things and change without panic and defensiveness.

3. Committed people tend to be people centered rather than issue-driven. They're not the sort of people whose minds are filled with a series of passionate bumper-sticker sayings which emerge from their mouths on all occasions.

4. Committed people see problems as deviations from the ideal and accept the challenge of making things right. They go about producing the ideal ends by a variety of problem-solving means, and are often more goal-oriented than means-driven or activity-bound. Uncommitted people are more likely to engage in activity for its own sake, to build great bureaucracies, and to cling to mindless procedures.

5. Committed people make up their own minds and are less apt

to be influenced by the lights of passing ships—by sales pitches, propaganda, con men, convention, and cant.

6. Committed people strive for personal growth; they're not seekers of the easy or comfortable deal. They're willing to pay the price to be bigger, smarter, and more skillful than they are now, and they find the price to be trivial in comparison to the rewards of such growth. Committed people are motivated not by their shortcomings but by the possibilities of being better.

Creative Goals Encourage Commitment

The establishment of creative goals plays an important role in getting people committed. Bosses who produce commitment in others usually encourage their people to be creative. Rather than punish innovation, they allow it or even demand it of their subordinates.

Creativity is a challenge which produces commitment in yourself and in your subordinates. Like David Sarnoff at RCA and Orville Beal at Prudential, Lee Iacocca generates such commitment to creativity at Chrysler today. Each of these leaders has recognized that people respond to the challenges by being creative in their own jobs.

A data-processing system can be used to maintain tight control, but it won't generate creativity. In fact, if that's the only face of management your people see, they lose autonomy and perhaps all interest in the work they are doing. Only when working on creative goals do people have the feeling that they are functioning at their highest level. They have no need then to seek conformity, popularity, or constant reminders to keep going at a pell-mell pace. You set your own pace when you are engaged in creative work.

Another reason why creative goals are important arises from the research of Gene Jennings, who found that creative goals have a way of producing more than enough energy to finish the job. Doing routine work and assigned activity according to procedural demands doesn't generate energy; it drains it.

Committed people often possess some vision which uncommitted people don't have.

Unlike the psychologists whose studies are focused upon disturbed minds, Abraham Maslow studied healthy-minded people who had experienced success in life. He found that a characteristic of these health-minded, committed, and successful people was the enjoyment of a kind of mystical experience which he described as "a peak experience."

Committed people tend to have more peak experiences in their lives than the uncommitted. These experiences are found in the shining hour when you look at your accomplishments and tell yourself: "This was one of my best achievements." Bosses who can get people working on things that produce more of these shining hours will get better results than bosses who are exacting, hostile, judgmental, and punitive.

Robert Browning once wrote of a journey that seemed endless until suddenly the towers of the city he was seeking emerged out of the mists and he could see the goal ahead. Then, even though the fog settled in once more, the dark path no longer seemed hopeless. With a vision of something good in front of you, the ordinary doesn't seem as dim or plain as it would without such a vision.

One of the nice things about being a social animal is that other people can lift up your vision of yourself and your condition. Bosses can assure us that there is a bigger meaning or higher goal than we presently see. Then, if we believe it, the drudgery becomes worthwhile and the long commute to work more bearable.

There are, however, some people who never see a vision, who never have a high moment to carry them over the valleys and the pits of their jobs. They don't want to see life this way. They would rather settle for a comfortable deal, a sinecure with high pay and no work. Such people live life in a rut (which is a grave with both ends open).

On the other hand, some people would like to live their entire lives camped out on these visionary heights. The problem with this is that you must pick some action plans to get going. The peak experiences we have are just marching orders. You have to put on your pack and start hiking, one step at a time, to get there. But the journey is exciting when the goal is clearly ahead.

If you want to turn your own job into a good job, my advice is to find some high moments and to devise a strategic plan for a victory or a big score. Then make a commitment to get there. Bear in mind that peak experiences aren't limited to such things as winning World War II. Opportunities for peak experiences and creativity exist in every job at every level of the organization.

Build Commitment among Staff People

It's apparent to anyone who spends any amount of time around government offices or those of large corporations that one of the major managerial problems is increasing the effectiveness of staff departments. The salaries of these staff people are at astonishingly high levels, by past standards. Many an ordinary staff person draws a salary of $50,000 a year or more today, and this adds up to an enormous overhead for many businesses. Many firms are cutting back on staff positions and sending people with many years of experience out onto the street. This often reflects the fact that many organizations simply fail to use their staff talent as fully as they might.

Unclear objectives and entanglement in bureaucratic procedures—as well as the lack of commitment which follows those conditions—have made the morale of staff people a major problem in many organizations. Getting staff people committed to important and exciting strategic goals is a major challenge to management. My impression is that many staff people have few, if any, peak experiences in their work. Their efforts are centered around surviving the cutbacks while keeping up their payments for tuition, mortgages, and the like. People whose major motivation is avoidance of being laid off are likely to be pretty deficient in commitment and in peak experiences.

What can you as a manager do to change this situation and to produce more commitment among staff people?

First, strategic goals need to be clarified and spelled out. The engineers, personnel specialists, purchasing agents, and accountants need big challenges and noble goals to bring out their best abilities. The payoff from setting some clear and exciting strategic goals is likely to be far more satisfying to the organization—and most certainly to its people—than any cost reduction program can ever be.

Second, strategic planning can't be limited to the few people at the top who must ultimately make the final stop-or-go decisions. The expertise of staff people at every level must be involved in the establishment of your strategic goals.

Third, long-range planning and strategic programs require more than overall goals. They require specific actions and means-testing by experts who have been let in on the visions of what is sought at the end of the trail.

Every staff department has some strategic consequences of its efforts, and those should be spelled out and hung up before the department's employees to gain their commitment.

As Frederick Herzberg pointed out years ago, the motivation of people is the key problem in managing organizations, and motivation means getting people committed to the pursuit of lofty goals, not the avoidance of bad things.

The search for commitment doesn't mean screening out the few people who have it from the many who don't. That wouldn't prove very productive. As Crawford Greenwalt, the former president of DuPont, put it, the biggest challenge to management is getting ordinary people to do extraordinary things. People who lack commitment become risk-avoiders, and nobody ever built a great organization with people who avoided the taking of risks.

The Knowledge Worker as a Special Case

In the world of service industry, where the typical worker is more likely to be a knowledge worker than a routine performer doing repetitive work, the possibility is always present that such people may withhold their best abilities. Studies by Lee Danielson, Don Pelz, and others many years ago at the University of Michigan showed the importance of motivation in engineers and scientists in their productivity, creativity, and general willingness to persist in the tortuous course of seeking new knowledge.

Engineering or scientific development often presses the knowledge worker against barriers of unknown technology where the productivity and success of the organization relies mainly upon the creativity, intelligence, technical experience, and persistence of the researcher. Unlike the people whose work is similar or identical from day to day, the creative person often works on one or two problems at a time in project form. To develop a new software program, to create a strategic plan, and to analyze economic data and produce a useful forecast may have important consequences for the survival, to say nothing of productivity and profit, of the firm or the attainment of public purposes in governmental or nonprofit agencies.

Human Factors in Project Management

When it comes to innovation, engineering, or research and development, many of the best people live in a world of project management. That's how such things get organized. For one thing, it simplifies the accounting, because the funds for projects usually come from a beneficent and critical daddy called a sponsor who puts up the money for a specific project, performed to the sponsor's specifications. The sponsor may not know exactly how the project will be done but usually has a very firm idea as to what the end results should be—and also a very firm budget idea, which is expressed in a contract.

This leaves the contractor with two major responsibilities (1) To figure out how to get to the sponsor's objectives, and (2) to do it within the agreed restraints of time and budget. Naturally this entails some risk for the contractor because technical obstacles might be encountered which weren't—or couldn't be—foreseen. Solving unforeseen problems in a timely fashion is important, not only to meet the project deadline but also to stay within budget. Although contract revisions may be negotiated, a contractor eventually eats the losses.

Thus, as a general rule, it's pretty important to be able to manage projects, and the best way to do so is by objectives. This basic conclusion reaches beyond the world of engineering and scientific research. Economic research, market research, computer program development, and consulting jobs of any type have the same two limits. Either you get the job done at the time promised and within the budget contracted for or you lose your shirt. Nevertheless there are a lot of people doing contract work who seldom if ever make their deadlines, which also means that cost overruns are produced. In plain English, their estimates weren't very accurate, and wrong estimates on contracts are rarely ever too high.

In applying to this process, to cure some of the system ills which seem to plague such highly technical work, we have to realize that the contract often is a promise to do something in the face of uncertainty and incomplete or imperfect information. There may be things which we simply don't know and can't find out until we've actually started on the project.

Project versus Program

In setting project management objectives, it's useful to identify two major categories: strategic and operational. The strategic we call a program, the operational we call a project. The program is usually a multiyear objective, and the project is a smaller portion which contributes one leg of the whole program. The program is likely to remain constant throughout its lifetime, although it might be cancelled outright before completion. The program is usually clear and simple to state, but horrendously difficult to execute. The project, on the other hand, might be broken down into dozens or even hundreds of subprojects. Each individual project is short-term in nature (likely to be accomplished in a single year), and with a high probability of success.

Project management really consists of laying out the various stages of the project in as much detail as is feasible and useful, with time and cost estimates for completion of each stage. PERT and CPM are tools for constructing charts which show what comes first and what occurs simultaneously and sequentially. But however necessary and useful these techniques may be, they don't get at the real problem which lies closer to the human factors involved—the organization and motivation of the people engaged in them.

Organizing for Project Management

If there is any orthodox or usual method of organization for project management it certainly must be the matrix form. This is a kind of organization plan which flies deliberately in the face of the old rule that a person should be responsible only to one boss. The matrix form of organization picks a project leader who in turn picks his or her team. The leader has responsibility for completion of the project but doesn't have authority over all of the people who must cooperate to get the various functions done. In short, you keep the functional organization intact with departments like manufacturing, sales, and personnel, which continue to perform their special functions.

Project managers have responsibility for completing a project on time and within budget, while home department are responsible for maintaining the administrative and production structure of the organization. Each pursues his or her own objectives, and occasionally these collide. Their priorities will differ and their rules for making things happen will conflict. As a result, negotiation and cooperation are very important, and bureaucratic rules for organizational functioning must often be set aside.

Making this complex system work requires human beings who possess sophisticated levels of interpersonal skills.

Good Objectives Produce "Objective Power"

The electricity went out in New York City a few years ago and all the regular services which depend upon electricity were out of commission. Street lights went dark, traffic lights stopped operating, and chaos loomed. But out of nowhere, all over the city, ordinary citizens began to pop out of the crowd and start directing traffic, which continued to flow in an orderly manner. Nobody was in charge, since the juice of civilized bureaucracy was lost. It was a kind of leaderless leadership which took over. The objective emerged from the emergency, and people responded spontaneously.

A similar occurrence took place recently in Bhopal, India, when a Union Carbide plant there spewed deadly gas into the city. Medical personnel moved swiftly to do what was needed to save thousands of live. As one doctor said, "Nobody was giving us order, so we just did what had to be done." The power of the objective made the tasks clear to the many people who had the ability to help.

Disasters and other emergency situations always seem to bring out the power of people to organize themselves to get the objective achieved, and this power continues to operate until the emergency is over. Then people lapse back into a more apathetic pattern, waiting for the bureaucratic organization to take over and exercise its decision-making authority.

In his terrific book *The Soul of a New Machine,* Tracy Kidder describes how a project group at Data General Corporation carried out the task of creating and debugging a new computer. Without the segmented and bureaucratic machinery which seems to characterize many industrial organizations, the engineers, programmers, and scientists plunged into the job, impelled by the objective. Long hours and personal inconvenience meant nothing, for the power of the objective gripped them all. When the project was completed, the team broke up. Many people left the firm, and others lapsed back into routine behavior.

Perhaps the biggest challenge for a project manager is that of hanging up a powerful objective before people who have the skills and tools to accomplish it. What accounts for this power of the objective?

1. The objective focuses energy from diversions which occupy people most of the time, and sets priorities for our time and our lives.

2. An exciting or noble goal generates commitment on the part of people; they adopt the goal as their very own.

3. Activity which is needed gets done while irrelevant activity fades away when people are clear on their objectives and committed to producing results.

4. People have a natural tendency to want to get things done once they have made personal commitments to an objective, and it's this personal commitment which is the primary source of the power of objectives.

Yet it's also possible to make a bureaucratic mess of objectives. Usually this occurs when people try to force the objectives to fit the formula of some procedural routine, or when the objectives become a bureaucratic series of mechanical steps to be followed in cookbook fashion.

The Role of Interpersonal Relationships

Each morning as you are preparing to go out to battle the world you make commitments to the face you see in the mirror. But when you actually get to work you often lose that determination and will to achieve. What produces this letdown? It might be the fact that the objectives you find in front of you at 9 a.m. when you walk into the lab or office aren't your own. They belong to somebody else, perhaps to some customer whose importance you question. Or maybe they were conceived by your boss, and you're not really certain that he or she has all of the words and music together logically. Or it may be that it's the objective of the organization which needs doing, and you have some reservations about whether this organization is really yours. Anyway, you stick it out and work on the objective because you have a mortgage, car payments, and some hefty tuition bills to pay. In even worse cases there may be no apparent reason for the work at all, or it may be so well hidden that you can't figure it out.

Many engineers, scientists, and staff people tell me that they don't have enough work to keep them busy, so they engage in make-work projects just in case anybody is watching. One young Cornell-trained engineer working for a large research organization near Boston recently confided to me that his boss seemed down on him because he was producing too much. You can bet that objective power wasn't present in any traceable quantity in that organization. But what produces objective power?

Having somebody out there whose opinion is important to you is the key ingredient, somebody such as a boss.

If you care about a person's good opinion and you make a commitment to that person to achieve some kind of objective, however large or small, you will focus your energy on delivering what you said you would deliver. Promises made demand that something be done about them, and objectives are promises made to somebody whose opinion is important.

Performers who get the feeling—either real or imagined—that they're being used by somebody for his or her own personal ends are not likely to become committed, and without commitment there is no objective power. That's where interpersonal skills come into play.

Every sponsor insists that there must be a single individual assigned as program manager for every contract or program and project. What the sponsor can't know is whether the project manager has the skill to get full commitment from the people who are doing the vital technical work on the project. This is the major function of the behavior of the project manager. Here are some guidelines:

1. A project manager who relies upon a title, rank, or big office to produce commitment will inevitably fail.

2. If the project manager doesn't build trust into the organization, commitment won't follow.

3. If the rules of the road, the purpose of the program, or the strategies being employed are changed without conferring with team members, commitment will be lost. After all, commitment is voluntary; it cannot be directed or ordered.

4. If the top management of the organization doesn't seem to be involved and to care about the outcome, it can hardly be expected that anybody else will be involved or care either.

5. If the project or program manager waffles on the level of caring about the project, it will falter.

6. If the project manager makes it clear that he or she has more important concerns and that the team members are really rather unimportant minions, their commitment dies. On the other hand, commitment flourishes when the project manager shows support and concern for people in their daily tasks.

7. If there is anything murky about a project's objectives, commitment will disappear and the project will fall behind schedule and go over budget.

8. A project manager who keeps switching people without giving clear reasons kills commitment.

To make things happen in work that calls for the support and commitment of a lot of different people, individual responsibilities must be defined clearly. It's sad to say, however, that such clearly defined responsibilities are far less common than one might suppose. Ask the average professional what his or her major project responsibilities are and you'll get one answer. Ask the project manager and you'll get another. The two sets of responsibilities will overlap by about 60 or 70 percent, but they will differ on the remaining 30 or 40 percent. Thus it isn't surprising that targets often don't get met.

Changes occur, of course, and you'll have to adapt your MBO system to fit the project management situation, but rapid or even occasionally radical change doesn't mean that objectives are useless. Just the opposite is true. Responsibilities have to be redefined every time a change occurs.

Project goals aren't determined by monthly accounting reports but by the dynamic and technical emergence of the project. Thus project managers must continually talk to their people about what's expected of them, what resources are available, how much freedom they have, and how much control is to be exerted.

During the mid-1950s I met Alfred P. Sloan, the retired president of General Motors, who was at that time working on his autobiography. When Mr. Sloan had a question about something of general interest in the book, he frequently would invite people to visit him so that he could pick their brains on the subject. At the time, I was manager of the personnel division of the American Management Association in New York. I was invited to meet with Mr. Sloan at his apartment in Manhattan. Sloan was a legendary figure, having served as president of General Motors for 28 years. I was delighted to meet him. He had also invited other so-called personnel experts, one from the Conference Board, another from Industrial Relations Counselors, and a couple of professors. The subject that Sloan wanted to discuss was this: Is it really possible for the large corporation and the individual employee of the corporation to have mutual interests which both can satisfy?

All of us optimistically assured him, "Of course they can, Mr. Sloan." But the question remains a nagging one. If the modern corporation can't operate in such a way that its employees can fulfill themselves, be whole human beings, functioning citizens of a democracy, good parents, family heads, and marriage partners, then the modern corporate society is possibly inherently unstable. Although Mr. Sloan was probably thinking more of the historical hostility between labor unions and management (he had been chief executive of General Motors during the famous sit-down strikes of 1937), his question is still pertinent for today's radically different work population.

Can the professionally educated and the highly talented white-collar worker survive and retain his or her intellectual and emotional maturity in a large organization? Can the modern worker's goals be integrated with those of today's organization? These questions pervade this book.

The waters are calm in union–management relations today, for the most part. Union membership is down, its militancy is muted, wages and benefits are sufficiently high that most unionized workers are members of the middle class. Their children go to college, they own their own homes, they have company-provided retirement benefits and health and life insurance. The situation appears less serene for many white-collar workers and professionals. Announcements that giant companies will "divest" 15 to 20 percent of their white-collar work force appear regularly in the business press. Banks, insurance companies, the textile industry, and manufacturers of durable goods and appliances are all under pressure to survive international competition and other problems. The professional career which was once undertaken for a lifetime now appears to last no longer than the will of the company.

Surveys show that the level of discontent in middle-management and white-collar professional jobs is higher than in many years. Consultant Clark Caskey suggests that there is "a mess in middle management." Mess or not, there is evidence of discontent. Is this a passing phase, or is Alfred Sloan's question even more meaningful today than it was when he asked it?

The question as I see it is how to *integrate* the needs, goals, aspirations, values, and hopes of professional workers with the goals and needs of the corporation or government organization. My confidence that they *can* be integrated remains firm, but only if management directs its affairs in ways that pay specific attention to those employee needs. It is not a zero-sum game; both can win, if we manage our human resources competently.

References

Albrecht, Karl. *Successful Management by Objectives*. Englewood Cliffs, N.J.: Prentice-Hall, 1978.

Barnard, Chester. *The Functions of the Executive*. Cambridge: Harvard University Press, 1938.

Beck, Arthur C., and Ellis D. Hillman. *Positive Management Practice*. San Francisco: Jossey Bass, 1985.

Bendix, Reinhard. *Max Weber: An Intellectual Portrait*. New York: Doubleday Anchor Books, 1962.

Berelson, Bernard, and George Steiner. *Human Behavior: An Inventory of Scientific Findings*. New York: Harcourt, Brace and World, 1964.

Blake, Robert. *The Versatile Manager*. Homewood, Ill.: Richard D. Irwin, 1981.

————, and Jane S. Mouton. *The Managerial Grid*. Houston: Gulf Publishing Co., 1954.

Brooks, Earl, and George S. Odiorne. *Managing by Negotiations*. New York: Van Nostrand Reinhold, 1984.

Davis, Ralph C. *The Fundamentals of Top Management*. New York: Harper and Row, 1951.

Drucker, Peter. *Management Tasks, Responsibilities, Structures*. New York: Harper and Row, 1974.

————. *The Practice of Management*. New York: Harper and Row, 1954.

Fiedler, Fred E. *A Theory of Leadership Effectiveness*. New York: McGraw-Hill, 1967.

Filley, Allen C., and Robert J. House. *Managerial Process and Organization Behavior*. Glenview, Ill.: Scott-Foresman, 1969.

Foyol, Henri. *Industrial and General Administration*. London: Pitman, 1949.

Gellerman, Saul W. *Management by Motivation*. New York: American Management Association, 1968.

Gilbert, Thomas F. *Competence: Engineering Worthy Performance*. New York: McGraw-Hill, 1978.

Goffman, E. *The Presentation of Self in Everyday Life*. New York: Doubleday, 1959.

Hartz, Peter. *Merger*. New York: William Morrow, 1985.

Huberman, John. "Discipline Without Punishment." *Harvard Business Review*, 1964.

Hughes, Charles. *Goal Setting*. New York: American Management Association, 1965.

Humble, John. *How to Manage by Objectives*. New York: American Management Association, 1972.

Jay, Anthony. *The Corporation Man*. New York: Random House, 1971.

Jennings, Eugene. *The Mobile Manager*. Ann Arbor: Bureau of Industrial Relations, University of Michigan, 1965.

Kidder, Tracy. *The Soul of a New Machine*. Boston, Mass. Atlantic Monthly Press, 1981.

Koontz, Harold, Cyril O'Donnell, and Heinz Weihrich. *Management*, 8th edition. New York: McGraw-Hill, 1984.

Kopelman, Richard E. *Managing Productivity in Organizations: A Practical, People Oriented Perspective*. New York: McGraw-Hill, 1986.

Lasch, Christopher. *The Culture of Narcissism*. New York: Warner Books, 1979.

Lehrer, Robert. *White Collar Productivity*. New York: McGraw-Hill, 1985.

Lewin, Kurt. "Intention, Will, and Need." In *Classics in Psychology*, edited by Thorne Shipley. New York: Philosophical Library, 1961.

Likert, Rensis. *New Patterns in Management*. New York: McGraw-Hill, 1961

Locke, Edward A. "The Relationship of Intentions to the Level of Performance." *Journal of Applied Psychology*, February 1966.

McClelland, David C. "Testing for Competence Rather Than for Intelligence." *American Psychologist*, January 1973.

Maccoby, Michael. *The Gamesman: The New Corporate Leaders*. New York: Simon and Schuster, 1976.

McConkey, Dale. *Management by Objectives for Staff Managers*. New York: Vantage, 1972.

MacDonald, Charles R. *MBO Can Work!* New York: McGraw-Hill, 1982.

McGregor, Douglas. *The Human Side of Enterprise*. New York: McGraw-Hill, 1960.

Mager, Robert F. *Goal Analysis*. Belmont, Calif.: Fearson Publishers, 1972.

Malek, Frederick V. *Washington's Hidden Tragedy*. New York: The Free Press, 1978.

Mali, Paul. *MBO Updated*. New York: Wiley Interscience, 1986.

Marvin, Philip. *The Right Man for the Right Job*. New York: Dow Jones Irwin, Inc., 1973.

Matheny, Philip. *Critical Path Hiring: How to Employ Top Flight Managers*. Lexington, Mass.: Lexington Books, 1986.

Merwin, John. "A Tale of Two Worlds." *Forbes*, June 16, 1986.

Mintzberg, Henry. *The Nature of Managerial Work*. New York: Harper and Row, 1973.

Odiorne, George S. *MBO II: A System of Managerial Leadership for the Eighties*. Belmont, Calif.: Fearon Pitman, 1979.

———. *Management and the Activity Trap.* New York: Harper and Row, 1972.

———. *Management by Objectives: A System of Managerial Leadership.* New York: Pitman, 1965.

———. "Mentoring: An American Management Innovation." *Personnel Administration,* May 1985.

———. *Strategic Management of Human Resources.* San Francisco: Jossey Bass, 1984.

———. *The Change Resisters.* Englewood Cliffs, N.J.: Prentice-Hall, 1981.

———. "The Great American Brain Drain." *Personnel Journal,* August 1985.

———. *Training by Objectives: An Economic Approach to Managment Training.* New York: Macmillan, 1970.

Patten, Thomas H., Jr. *A Manager's Guide to Performance Appraisal.* New York: The Free Press, 1982.

Peters, Thomas J., and Robert H. Waterman, Jr. *In Search of Excellence: Lessons from America's Best-Run Companies.* New York: Harper & Row, 1982.

Raia, Anthony P. *Managing by Objectives.* Glenview, Ill.: Scott, Foresman, 1974.

Reddin, William. *Effective Management by Objectives.* New York: McGraw-Hill, 1971.

Reichel, Arie. "The Declining Level of Trust in American Corporations." Ph.D. dissertation, University of Massachusetts, 1980.

Roethlisberger, F. J., and William S. Dickson. *Management and the Worker.* Cambridge: Harvard University Press, 1940.

Ryan, T. A. *Work and Effort.* New York: McGraw-Hill, 1956.

Siegel, Irving H. *Company Productivity: Measurement for Improvement.* Kalamazoo: Upjohn Institute for Employment Research, 1980.

Skinner, B. F. *Science and Human Behavior.* New York: Macmillan 1953.

———, and James Holland. *The Analysis of Behavior.* New York: McGraw-Hill, 1961.

Smith, Robert E. *Workrights.* New York: E.P. Dutton, 1983.

Sobel, Robert. *The Entrepreneurs.* New York: Weybright and Talley, 1974.

Tannenbaum, Robert, and W.H. Schmidt. "How to Choose a Leadership Pattern." *Harvard Business Review,* March–April 1958.

Toffler, Alvin. *The Third Wave.* New York: Bantam Books, 1980.

Wanous, J.P., *Organizational Entry Recruitment: Selections and Socialization of Newcomers.* Reading, Mass.: Addison Wesley, 1980.

Index

Top management (*continued*)
31; cultural lag of, 172; goal
setting by, 70–72, 76
Trade-offs required by goal setting,
37, 84–89
Training, 118–120, 130–140; access
to, 148–149; action training
techniques, 116, 124; behavioral
focus of, 112–113; budget for,
107; commitment to, 107, 170;
criteria for, 114–115; determining
need for, 114, 127; engaging
outside speakers for, 124–126;
evaluation of, 117–118; facilities,
119–120; for first-line
management, 18; human relations,
58; in-house, 123–126; outside,
120–123; MBA, 174; in goal
setting, 76–77; motivation and,
110; to nurture risk takers, 80; on-
the-job reinforcement of, 124;
performance appraisal, 31;
retraining, 111–112, 129; in
service organizations, 175–176;
simulation, 115; stages, 116;
technological updating, 20; ten
guides to excellence in, 112–118;
as tool of integration, 107–126;
for workhorse employees, 132,
133–135
Trollope, Anthony, 185
Truman, Harry, 48
Trust, 218; bait-and-switch
management and, 42–43; building,
40, 45–46, 98–99
Trustee, manager as, 8–11
Type A behavior, 151

"Understudy method" of supervision.
See Mentoring
"Uneasy Look at Performance
Review, An" (McGregor), 30
Union Carbide, 215
Unions, 160; foreign competition and,
50; management relations with,
xii; manager as trustee for, 9

United States: balance of payments,
173; productivity of, 166–167
U.S. Congress, 44, 206
U.S. Department of Commerce, 172
U.S. Department of Labor, 128
U.S. Justice Department, 87
US Steel, 49

Value(s): adding, 171; clarification,
22; of women and minorities, 18
Vengeful employees, 159–163
Veterans' Administration, 63

W.T. Grant, 3, 61
Wage give-backs, 50
Waterman, Robert, Jr., 138–139, 189
Weaknesses, assessment of, 65–66
Weber, Max, 13
Wells Fargo Bank, 4
Western Electric, Hawthorne plant of,
5–6
White-collar productivity committee,
182
White-collar workers, 128; discontent
among, xii; "divesting" of
segments of, xii; prevalence of, 17;
productivity, 177–182
Women: expectations of, 130;
mentoring problems for, 193–194,
195; values of, 18
Work force. *See* Human resources
Work habits, poor, 151–152
Workhorses: concentration on, 25–
26; contribution of, 136–137;
managing of, 135–138, 139–140;
motivation of, 137–138, 142;
supervisor category, 131; training,
132, 133–135
Wrapp, Edward, 8

Xerox, 63, 112

About the Author

G EORGE S. ODIORNE is The Harold D. Holder Professor of Management at Eckerd College, St. Petersburg, Florida. Prior to joining Eckerd College, he was a professor and dean of the School of Business Administration at the University of Massachusetts at Amherst, dean of the College of Business and professor of management at the University of Utah, and director of the Bureau of Industrial Relations at the University of Michigan. He has also taught management and economics at Rutgers University and New York University. His business experience includes managerial positions with General Mills, Inc., the American Management Association, and American Can Company. He has served as a consultant to major American corporations. He received a B.A. from Rutgers University, an M.B.A. and Ph.D. from New York University, and an honorary doctorate from Central New England University.

Dr. Odiorne serves on the board of directors of several corporations and civic institutions, and he is a member of several learned societies. He is listed in *Who's Who in America* and *American Men of Science*, and he is a member of the National Management Association Hall of Fame. Dr. Odiorne is the author of twenty-three books and over three hundred articles. His books include *Management by Negotiations* (1984), *Strategic Management of Human Resources* (1984), *Techniques of Organization Change* (1983), *Sales Management by Objectives* (1982), *The Change Resisters* (1981), *Personal Effectiveness* (1980), *MBO II: A System of Managerial Leadership* (1979), *Management and the Activity Trap* (1974), *Personnel Administration* (1972), *Green Power: Corporations and the*

Urban Crisis (1969), and *Management Decisions by Objectives* (1969). His books have been translated into eight different languages. He is also author of the *George Odiorne Letter*, a bimonthly letter on executive skills, which is read by executives in eleven nations.